THE TEA BOOK

THE TEA BOOK

all things tea
Louise Cheadle
and Nick Kilby of
teapigs.

STERLING EPICURE
New York

STERLING EPICURE
New York

An Imprint of Sterling Publishing
1166 Avenue of the Americas
New York, NY 10036

STERLING EPICURE is a trademark of Sterling
Publishing Co., Inc. The distinctive Sterling logo is a
registered trademark of Sterling Publishing Co., Inc.

Text copyright © 2015 teapigs Limited

Produced by Jacqui Small LLP

Illustrated by Emma Cobb, Jitesh Patel,
Will Scobie, and Vicki Turner

Food photographed by Charlotte Tolhurst

Illustrations © 2015 Sterling Publishing,
except on pages 20–21, 34–35, 40–41, 46–47, 52–53
and 70–71 © Jitesh Patel 2015

ISBN 978-1-4549-1718-2

Distributed in Canada by Sterling Publishing
c/o Canadian Manda Group, 664 Annette Street
Toronto, Ontario, Canada M6S 2C8

For information about custom editions, special sales,
and premium and corporate purchases, please contact
Sterling Special Sales at 800-805-5489 or specialsales@
sterlingpublishing.com.

Manufactured in China
2 4 6 8 10 9 7 5 3 1

www.sterlingpublishing.com

Tea-smoked duck breasts with
spiced pears and Old Williamsburg
mandarin tea © Lindy Wildsmith
Earl Grey hearts © Hearst Magazines
Ltd and Jacqui Small LLP
Green tea pound cake and Jewish
honey cake © Roger Pizey
Tea loaf © Jane Brocket
Matcha and chocolate shortbread
© William Curley
Black currant tea and chocolate
truffle ice cream © David Lebovitz
Almond iced tea and Matcharita
© Tom Sandham
Iced tea lollies; Sipsmith super fruit
sundowner; Supereasy, real, freshly
brewed iced teas; "Knock your socks
off" tea shakes; Matcha coconut tea
shake; All-natural chai and matcha
lattes; and Super-power matcha
smoothies © teapigs Limited
All other recipes © Jacqui Small

Some recipes recommend particular
blends of tea; if these are difficult
to find, you can make the recipes
using other whole leaf mesh bags or
loose leaf tea, but you may need to
experiment with the amount as the
strength of flavor may well vary.

Contents

Introduction

Welcome to our book about tea. We are Louise Cheadle and Nick Kilby, the founders of teapigs. Hello! It's nice to meet you.

As self-confessed tea nuts, we have always been and will always be crazy for anything related to tea. The kettle and the teapot (and more recently the mug) have been part of our lives, so much so that we both have made our living in the world of tea. We've been lucky enough to travel the world and sample all sorts of varieties of tea and, more importantly, experience the deep meaning that tea has in so many contrasting cultures.

In 2006 we took the big step to found a new tea company, teapigs. We're based in the UK where tea is the national drink with a long history. However, we thought it was time to revisit some of the traditions associated with drinking tea and bring it into the 21st century. So, we launched our "tea temples" (quality whole leaf tea in a convenient pyramid mesh bag) and we haven't looked back since. We love tea; we love its history and origins. But what we love most is its future—a drink that can excite and bring people together worldwide. In this book, we've tried to capture some of the things that make tea so special to us. We'll take you on a brief tour around the world to highlight just how global this lovely drink really is and the role it plays in many cultures. A brief history (we could have written a few books on the history of tea but that's not our style) helps to put in context why tea has become such a widespread favorite around the world. Then, we'll hold your hand and take you on a journey to meet all the differing styles of tea, show you how they are produced, and give you an opportunity to meet some of the people who produce them. Followed by letting you in on the secrets of making the perfect cup of tea, best cookies to dunk, and tea etiquette. Thrown in along the way, you'll find fun facts and we round off with some recipes all involving our favorite beverage.

We hope you like reading this book as much as we've enjoyed writing it.

Nick, Louise

This page, clockwise from above Turkish mint tea; Indian chai wallah; and tea harvest in Darjeeling.

Opposite, clockwise from top left Tea decorations (Rouen, France); tea plantation in Kerala, India; a happy English tea drinker, circa 1951; a happy Arabian tea drinker; and fresh, organic iced tea at Borough Market, London, UK.

CROP IMAGES TO FIT

Opposite, clockwise from top left Spice tea market, India; tea for sale Gantok, India; tea for sale Lille, France; and rickshaw wallah, Kolkata (formerly Calcutta), India.

This page, clockwise from above left The rolling room, Norwood Estates, Sri Lanka; tea pluckers in Thailand; teapots at the Golestan Inn Guesthouse, Kashan, Iran; and enjoying chai in Daushuar village, just outside Kaziranga National Park, Assam, India.

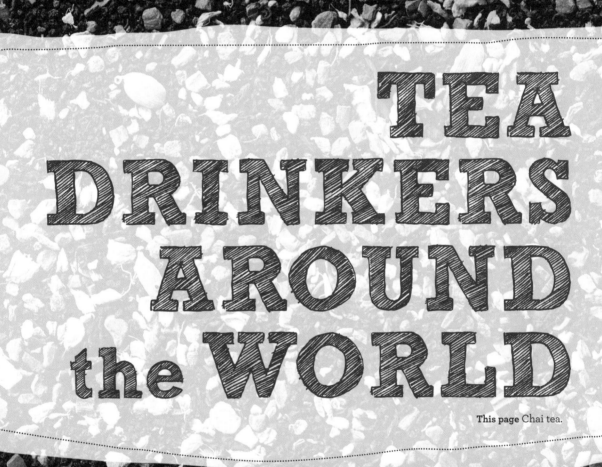

TEA DRINKERS AROUND the WORLD

This page Chai tea.

A world of tea drinkers

The humble little tea leaf has made quite an impact worldwide. In fact, it's become the second most drunk beverage in the world after, not surprisingly, water. So, forget those fizzy, sugary soft drinks, those beers and wines that'll leave you with a headache, and that other hot, black liquid (which can make you jittery), it's tea that's the planet's real hero.

Tea unites the world. It's drunk to bring people together, to calm us down, to pep us up, to soothe a crisis, and to celebrate a reunion. It's drunk out of mugs, cups, glasses, and saucers; it's drunk hot or iced, with spices, with sugar, with honey, with fruit, with milk (of all sorts: yak, we hear, is special), without milk, with, well, whatever really takes your fancy. Learning to make tea is like a rite of passage and, of course, only you can make yourself the perfect cup. There are ceremonies the world over to celebrate the making of our favorite drink. Over the following pages we explore some of the customs and traditions of tea drinking worldwide and highlight how this amazing drink has such a deep but diverse cultural following.

By the mid-18th century, tea had leapfrogged gin to claim the title of **BRITAIN**'s favorite drink.

IRELAND may be famed for its beloved Guinness, but its people drink more tea per day than any other European nation!

NEW YORK is believed to be the birthplace of the tea bag in 1908—a tea merchant inadvertently invented it when he wrapped up his tea samples in silk bags to help keep them safe in transit.

Mint tea is a staple of **MOROCCAN** hospitality—if you're ever offered a cup from a local, be sure to accept as refusing is seen as extreme rudeness. Take 5 minutes to sit down, relax, and enjoy!

Yerba mate, an indigenous plant from the Amazon jungle, is the massive favorite hot brew in **ARGENTINA** and **URUGUAY**.

Tea in **RUSSIA** is traditionally made in a samovar —a type of urn used to boil water that has a teapot filled with tea concentrate on the top.

SIBERIA used solid blocks of tea as a currency until the 19th century.

The beautifully pink brew of noon chai is extremely popular in the region of **KASHMIR**.

Butter tea is the drink of choice in **TIBET**—tea churned with yak's butter and salt may not be to everyone's taste, but it gives just the right amount of energy to cope with life in the Himalayas.

In **MYANMAR**, they have an entirely different way to enjoy tea—they pickle it to create *lahpet*!

TAIWAN gave us bubble tea and we are forever grateful!

When in **IRAN** do as the locals do and pop a sugar cube in your mouth before taking a sip of hot tea—definitely one for anyone with a sweet tooth to try!

The tea industry in **INDIA** employs over 1 million people.

HONG KONG offers the amazingly nicknamed "pantyhose milk tea"—a mixture of black tea and condensed milk that has been passed through a sackcloth bag, which just so happens to look an awful lot like ladies' hosiery! Yum!

In **SOUTH AFRICA** rooibos (or "redbush tea"), from the mountainous Cederberg region, is a favorite drink, usually drunk without milk but with lemon or honey.

In **AUSTRALIA** they "billy up the fire" to make billy tea, made famous by the swagman in the lyrics to *Waltzing Matilda*.

Who knew?

The world over, tea has its name synonymous with the country you're in. It seems that in those countries where tea arrived by ship the words for tea begin with the letter "t"—for instance *tee* (German), *thé* (French), and *té* (Spanish)—while those countries where it arrived overland use words beginning with "tch" or "ch"—*çay* (Turkish), *chay* (Russian), *chai* (Arabic and in India), and *po cha* (Tibetan)— from the Mandarin "cha."

TOP 20 TEA GUZZLERS

TURKEY
6.48lb/2.937kg

IRELAND
4.74lb/2.151kg

UZBEKISTAN
4.55lb/2.062kg

UNITED KINGDOM
3.66lb/1.661kg

PAKISTAN
3.31lb/1.501kg

KAZAKHSTAN
3.31lb/1.500kg

RUSSIA
2.98lb/1.350kg

TUNISIA
2.73lb/1.238kg

MOROCCO
2.58lb/1.170kg

NEW ZEALAND
2.57lb/1.165kg

When it comes to knocking back our favorite brew, it's Turkey that comes out on top when measured on how much a person drinks. Basically, that means the Turkish get through more tea per person than any other country in the world. We raise our glasses (of tea, of course) to their good taste.

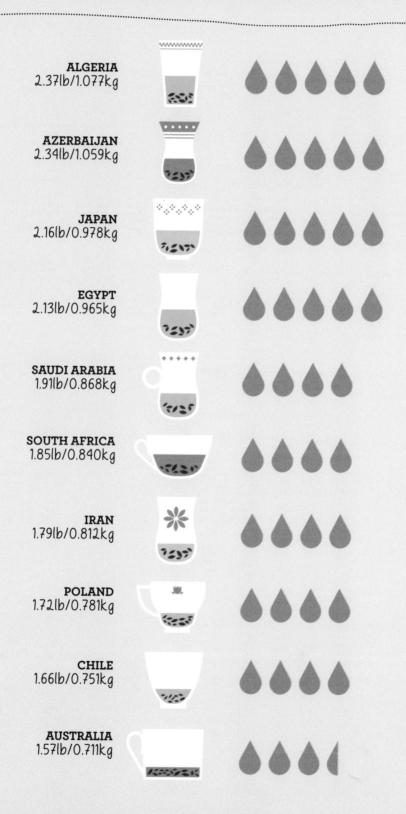

ALGERIA
2.37lb/1.077kg

AZERBAIJAN
2.34lb/1.059kg

JAPAN
2.16lb/0.978kg

EGYPT
2.13lb/0.965kg

SAUDI ARABIA
1.91lb/0.868kg

SOUTH AFRICA
1.85lb/0.840kg

IRAN
1.79lb/0.812kg

POLAND
1.72lb/0.781kg

CHILE
1.66lb/0.751kg

AUSTRALIA
1.57lb/0.711kg

(ALL DATA FROM EUROMONITOR 2013)

TOP 20 TEA DRINKERS

CHINA
1,216,909lb/548,043kg

INDIA
891,020lb/401,277kg

PAKISTAN
616,862lb/277,808kg

TURKEY
494,601lb/222,747kg

RUSSIA
431,636lb/194,390kg

JAPAN
275,904lb/124,255kg

INDONESIA
250,382lb/112,761kg

UK
234,197lb/105,472kg

EGYPT
178,598lb/80,433kg

While the Turkish drink the most individually, China comes out as the top tea-drinking nation—consuming the most lb/kg of tea per year. That means that more tea is drunk in China than in any other country. China does have a bit of an unfair advantage, though, as its population is pretty big.

USA
162,438lb/73,155kg

IRAN
141,399lb/63,680kg

UZBEKISTAN
134,289lb/60,478kg

GERMANY
127,865lb/57,585kg

ALGERIA
95,478lb/42,999kg

SOUTH AFRICA
93,213lb/41,979kg

MOROCCO
87,020lb/39,190kg

POLAND
66,767lb/30,069kg

BANGLADESH
64,640lb/29,111kg

UKRAINE
59,164lb/26,645kg

SAUDI ARABIA
56,637lb/25,507kg

(ALL DATA FROM EUROMONITOR 2013)

Northern Europe

Tea "hit" Northern Europe way back in the 17th century—just one of the many new and interesting products that were arriving from Asia as a result of the trading routes being opened up by the Dutch and Portuguese. Its influence and popularity gradually spread, mostly among the aristocracy as it commanded a high price. Over time, though, as supply became greater and taxes lower, the tea-drinking habit spread to a wider audience and became rooted in the culture of certain countries, none more so than in Great Britain.

GREAT BRITAIN

So, how do you take your tea? Well, that's a pretty common question in Britain as the population manages to drink its way through 165 million cups of tea everyday. That's an amazing 115,000 cups a minute or nearly 2,000 cups a second! Whether they're drinking tea out of a chipped mug with milk and sugar or sipping Earl Grey from the finest bone china teacup, the British have a relationship with tea that is cemented into its culture. It's the fixer in any situation, the "social glue" that keeps the country running. Imagine taking tea away from the Brits? The country would come to a standstill; there would be revolution in the air. Nothing to calm down those in a crisis. Nothing to lubricate the throat when gossiping with friends. What would happen to the cookie industry? What would be said to the vicar when he/she visits?

Britain's relationship with tea started in the 1600s (more of that later on, see page 83) when it was seen as a very aristocratic drink. Compare that to today when pretty much everyone in the country enjoys tea in their own personal and special way.

While the traditional cup of black tea with milk (and maybe a sugar cube or two) is still by far the most popular way of drinking tea, more and more people are now wetting their lips with more exotic teas. We see green teas, white teas, oolong, lapsang souchong, pu-erh tea, Matcha, and single-estate teas. Fruit and herbal teas (not strictly tea as they don't come from the *Camellia sinensis* plant; see also page 90) have become popular especially with younger tea drinkers who enjoy the myriad of flavor sensations. We also see more interesting ways of drinking tea; freshly brewed iced teas and chai lattes are becoming popular. Bubble tea, a rather strange combination of tea, fruit, and tapioca balls can now be found in the "cooler" places around. So, it appears that the British love affair with tea is still strong and will continue for years to come, even if some of the traditional etiquette may be on the wane. Pinkies out!

TEA LEAVES PREDICT THE FUTURE The British have certainly fallen in love with the tea bag. First commercially introduced by Tetley in 1953, the tea bag now completely dominates tea making with 96% of all tea being made from a tea bag. One unfortunate result of this has been the demise of the custom of "reading the tea leaves." In the past, most tea was made in a teapot with loose tea. Tea was poured into a cup or mug, without a strainer, and after the tea was drunk (watch out for the leaves) the cup was given a final swirl, resulting in the leaves forming a pattern of some sorts at the bottom of the cup. The "diviner" or tea-leaf reader then got to work attempting to predict the future of the drinker by interpreting the patterns left by the tea leaves. There were even tables produced to help interpret the leaves. Once the reading was done, the leaves were simply rinsed down the drain. A bit like flushing your future away.

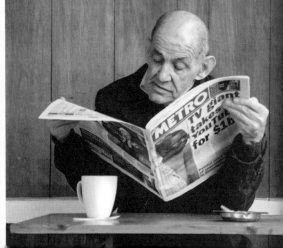

FROM TEASHOPS TO THE TEASMADE

Britain's rich history in tea has led to some very unique tea-related customs:

TEA SHOPS

In 1864, the Aerated Bread Company (ABC) started serving tea and snacks to its customers creating in effect Britain's first teashop. What was remarkable about these teashops was that they were the only places at the time where unaccompanied ladies could meet with friends without damaging their reputations. The teashop concept really took off, with ABC teashops spreading across the nation. They were rivaled by J Lyons & Co. who built a nationwide chain of over 250 stores and a smaller number of grander corner houses: larger establishments that contained numerous restaurants with musical entertainment. Changing social and eating habits led to the demise of teashops. Of course, today every main street is inundated by coffee shops. Will we ever see the return of the teashop? We hope so. Let's make it happen!

The Teasmade

In a country where "everything stops for tea" an obvious invention is a machine that will wake you up in the morning with a steaming cup by your bedside (the tea's made, get it?!). Early patents for such a machine can be traced back to the late 1800s but it was not until the 1930s that commercial machines first started to appear. By the midsixties no wedding list was complete without a Teasmade. Numerous makes and models sat on bedside tables across Britain, primed to make a steaming hot cup of tea in conjunction with a wake-up alarm. Before going to bed the lucky recipient would fill the pot with tea, the kettle with water, and set the alarm. The timer sets the kettle to boil, the boiling water passes to the pot, the tea brews, and the alarm wakes the sweetly dreaming tea lover. All that's left is to pour the tea and add milk and sugar, to taste. Genius!

TEA BREAKS

Long days toiling the land or working in factories would traditionally be broken up by a midmorning and a midafternoon tea break. Despite efforts by industrialists, landowners, and clerics, who tried to put a stop to them, the tea break became almost a national institution. The tea break also led to the role of the tea lady, usually the "unsung hero" of any office who would ensure a supply of tea and cookies to the workforce, often served from a trolley whose centerpiece would be a huge tea urn for boiling water. Sadly, with the introduction of vending machines and changing working attitudes, the tea lady has almost become part of the folklore of tea history in Britain.

tea dances

Back in the early 1700s a popular form of entertainment were events held in public gardens where people would gather to meet, watch entertainers, dance, and drink tea; these places were known as pleasure gardens or tea gardens. Many famous gardens in London, such as those in Vauxhall and Ranelagh, were popular venues for such events. Dancing and drinking tea became fashionable and the tea dance was born. People enjoyed tea dances well into the mid-20th century. But when popular culture changed dramatically in the 1960s, the tea dance declined in popularity; that said, they have made something of a return in recent years as people look to enjoy traditions from the past and discover the joy of dancing and, of course, drinking tea.

IRELAND

We like the Irish. They take tea seriously, just like us; in fact, tea is on a par with their beloved Guinness. And the Irish should know a thing or two about their brew as they drink more cups of tea per capita than any other country in the world, except Turkey (see page 18)—the average is four cups a day but many people drink six or more (see also page 18). However many cups are drunk, though, the recipe for an Irish cup of tea—or "cupan tae" as it is in Gaelic—is the same: one part milk to two parts tea. And milk has to go in the cup or mug first, not after.

Back in the early 1800s, tea in Ireland was only for the upper class but within 50 years or so, everyone on the Emerald Isle was drinking tea; it was a valuable commodity and was often bartered for eggs and milk in rural areas. That said, the tea on offer was often really poor quality, so, to make this tea more palatable lots of milk and sugar was added to the strongly brewed tea leaves.

Even today, the tea imported, sold, and brewed in Ireland is a bold blend drunk as a strong brew. Most Irish teas are strong black blends, predominantly Assam either alone or blended with Ceylon or East African teas (see also pages 120, 124–128, 130, and 132).

Above National treasures: Guinness and tea signs for sale in a secondhand shop.

 Who knew?

Tea first, or milk? The perennial question remains, despite scientific research that has never conclusively come up with an answer. The origins of milk first apparently relate back to the days when hot tea was poured into very fine bone china. Putting milk in first helped prevent the porcelain cups from breaking.

Probably one of the most famous and enduring tea traditions associated with Britain is the custom of taking afternoon tea. We have Anna, the 7th Duchess of Bedford, to thank for this treat as she thought up the idea of filling the void between breakfast and dinner by drinking tea late in the afternoon accompanied by a wondrous variety of savory and sweet snacks. There are all sorts of places to "take" afternoon tea nowadays; and GB and Ireland has a great variety to keep everyone happy.

THE RITZ HOTEL
150 Piccadilly, London W1J 9BR
www.theritzlondon.com
If you want the full-blown afternoon tea experience and be safe in the knowledge that no one around you is wearing sneakers, you'll be glad to hear there are lots of hotels keeping the formal tradition alive. Most famously of all, The Ritz offers a divine afternoon tea every day, complete with pianist, harpist, or string quintet! The setting is beyond compare, making it the perfect destination to take visiting relatives, celebrate a special occasion, or simply treat yourself to a fancy Wednesday afternoon tea … because, why not?!

BETTYS TEA ROOMS
Six locations around Yorkshire
www.bettys.co.uk
Bettys Tea Rooms offer an all-round classic afternoon tea. With a glowing reputation, thanks to many years of experience, they offer up a fresh pot of tea alongside delightful sandwiches, handmade cakes, and fresh scones (with Yorkshire clotted cream!). Each

Who knew?
The British are known for dunking cookies in their tea. Recent research by Dr. Stuart Farrimond concluded that the length of time a cookie can be dunked is roughly proportional to the amount of fat and sugar in a cookie. The Rich Tea cookie was declared the best for dunking.

Right Drink, Shop & Do.

of their six locations is set within a charming historic building.

AQUA SHARD
Level 31 The Shard, 31 St. Thomas Street, London SE1 9RY
www.aquashard.co.uk
If you're on a tight schedule and like ticking two things off your "London must-do" list, why not book yourself a table for tea at Aqua Shard? There you can enjoy the finest tea offerings; exquisite food, and gaze over London's breathtaking views while being 31 floors up London's tallest building. Tea and sightseeing all in one—perfect!

DRINK, SHOP & DO
9 Caledonian Road, London N1 9DX
www.drinkshopdo.com
In recent years more and more establishments have veered away from the traditional image of afternoon tea in a bid to inject life into the British classic. Afternoon tea has become more of an all-round experience, and by doing so has captivated a younger audience. Drink, Shop & Do in London is a classic example of this—on the weekend, they offer an "afternoon tea and do" session where you can choose either a classic or a boozy afternoon tea and the opportunity to make something to take home with you. Whether you choose a flower headband, hair fascinator, garters, or jewelry it's a great chance to get together with your pals, enjoy some tea, and get crafty!

LEAF
65–67 Bold Street, Liverpool L1 4EZ
www.thisisleaf.co.uk
Leaf offers a far more edgy approach to afternoon tea. Starting out life as a friendly independent teashop with a fab selection of teas, they soon saw a gap in the market and developed into a space where you can also enjoy art, vintage markets, bands as well as having regular club nights.

TEA GARDEN
7 Lower Ormond Quay, Dublin 1
www.tea-garden.eu
The Tea Garden is the kind of place you want to find yourself on a rainy afternoon in Dublin. Its cushioned floor, candlelit tables, and gorgeously tranquil atmosphere make it the perfect hideaway to shelter from the elements or escape hectic city life. They offer an incredibly broad range of teas to enjoy, as well as a separate menu of loose teas to buy and take home to enjoy. A true hidden gem, and a must for anyone looking for a relaxing vibe complete with stunning tea.

SWEDEN, NORWAY, AND DENMARK

It's difficult to tell when tea drinking began but it seems that the Vikings drank tea (whether it was out of their helmets or not is another matter). It was likely to be a herbal concoction made from angelica, birch, and moss. These days Northern European countries have a predominant culture of coffee drinking, but tea is now really catching on in the numerous coffee shops that can be found in the Nordic countries. Tea, particularly green teas, and herbal infusions are seen as a more relaxing and healthy alternative to coffee. Large "tins" of tea adorn the walls of many coffee shops and teas are generally served in glasses to show off the lovely colors of the various blends. No milk required.

Who knew?

In Sweden, there is a culture of social coffee breaks known as "fika" where people stop work or whatever else they're doing to gather to have nibbles and coffee —but tea is always an option! Fika is both a verb and a noun as it's so embedded in their culture.

THE NETHERLANDS

So, it was actually the Dutch we have to thank for bringing the first tea to Europe, in 1610 to be precise, a green tea from Japan. The Dutch East India Company were hugely successful traders and importers of tea throughout the 17th century. The future King of England, Charles II, gained a liking for tea while in exile at The Hague. Sadly for the Dutch their early dominance in trading with Asia gradually declined to the point where it was driven out altogether. But tea is still a popular drink in the numerous coffee shops with a broad range of teas, fruit teas, and herbal concoctions available.

Nowadays, you may associate coffee shops with the Netherlands but you are just as likely to be offered tea. Don't worry if you order tea and a glass or porcelain beaker of boiling water is brought to your table, it'll be followed swiftly by a selection box of tea bags in all flavors imaginable, so that you can choose and then steep your bag (be it a dusty one or not) to your own liking. But if you are partial to milk in your tea, you'll have to make a special request as the Dutch tend to drink their tea weak and black.

Above left Chaikhanna teashop, Gamla Stan, Stockholm, Sweden.

GREENWOODS
Keizersgracht 465,
1017 DK Amsterdam
www.greenwoods.eu

With its English name, it's not surprising that Greenwoods was created to be the Netherlands capital's first full-on English tearoom, and after its instant success with the locals and tourists alike, it has been something of an institution ever since. They offer a fantastic selection of premium loose-leaf teas from Van Geels & Co as well as a selection of superb Grand Cru loose-leaf teas from De Eenhorn—there really is something for everyone. The tearoom itself is gorgeously designed and carefully furnished to create the most relaxing atmosphere possible. Whether you're popping in to fuel up for a long day of exploring (we say, go for the eggs Benedict!) or to seek a few moments of solace it really is a treasured spot and definitely worth a visit, or two. In fact, you can even rent the apartment upstairs!

FORMOCHA PREMIUM TEA
Brouwersgracht 282, 1013 HG
Amsterdam
www.formocha.nl

We can't urge you enough to visit this beautiful establishment located in the heart of Amsterdam—a true tea-lover's paradise! Formocha is the Netherlands' first and only Chinese teahouse and offers an incredible range of carefully chosen specialty loose-leaf Chinese teas. Even on your first visit you are welcomed as though you are a close friend by the charming and knowledgeable owner, warmly invited to sit, relax, and enjoy some of the best tea to be found in the city. As far as teahouses go, Formocha is otherworldly and manages to create such a calming environment it would be easy to while away hours in this teacentric utopia. If you find yourself wandering the streets of Amsterdam one afternoon then do make a tea stop here.

A. C. PERCH'S TEA MERCHANTS
Kronprinsensgade 5, 1114
Copenhagen K
www.perchs.dk

Tea is trendy in Denmark. For some it might be hard to believe that a

tiny, unassuming old-fashioned shop, crammed with every imaginable sort of tea could be so enchanting—but it truly is! The shop is reminiscent of an old apothecary, with jars of loose-leaf tea everywhere you look and enthusiastic staff ready and waiting to measure out your tea of choice on gorgeous brass scales. As if the shop wasn't enough of a visual treat, there is also an adjoining tearoom where you can experience the tea in all its glory as well as indulge in a slice of cake or even one of their high tea options!

DAC& CAFE
Strandgade 27B,
1401 Copenhagen K
www.dac.dk

It won't take you too long to stumble across one of the many tearooms in Copenhagen, but why not head straight for this place—a small café within the Danish Architecture Centre? It may not seem like the most obvious place to stop for tea, but bear with me here! The building itself almost appears out of nowhere and is a welcome refuge for those who have spent hours wandering around the city to find themselves on "the wrong side of the harbor." But fear not, the café serves a number of great meals as well as lovely individual pots of tea! Be sure to grab yourself a spot in the glass balcony, where you'll have gorgeous views of the city and rejoice in the almost hypnotic task of watching the boats come and go. Plus, on the other side of the harbor are Copenhagen's infamous sidewalk trampolines—that's hours of fun right there, watching people jump around.

AM SWEET
rue des Chartreux 4,
1000 Brussels

An utterly charming, family-owned tearoom located behind a quaint wooden façade, this Belgian hidden gem in the heart of Brussels is treasured by locals and tourists alike. Here they offer a vast selection of Mariage Frères tea as well as a number of divine cakes and pastries. Whether you're after a quick cup of tea or a place to spend a lovely afternoon, AM Sweet's tearoom provides an incredible cozy and welcoming atmosphere that

will make you never want to leave. That said, space is tight, but there are a number of small wooden tables adding to the authentic charm of this place— if you manage to grab one of the cozy couches upstairs, then you really are one of the lucky few! As if this place wasn't charming enough, the owners even let their gorgeous dog wander freely around the café—all they ask is that you don't feed him treats, but sometimes it is incredibly hard to resist.

PEPPER MINT TEA ROOM
11 rue des Grands Carmes,
1000 Brussels

Located on a beautiful little cobbled side street, this Belgian tearoom offers a wonderful little hideaway for those wishing to escape the hustle and bustle of the Grand Place. It's easy to miss this unassuming shop, but the friendly welcome from the owner and the cozy and familiar atmosphere make it somewhere that's definitely worth a visit. This is the perfect spot to unwind with a brunch, light lunch, and a pot of specialty tea from around the world.

Below Greenwoods café, Amsterdam.

GERMANY

Sharing a border with Holland meant that tea was available in Germany not long after arriving on European soil. The first tea was used as a medicinal but within 100 years had become a popular and widespread drink—it even overtook home-brewed beer! Tea in Germany has always been highly valued, twice being subject to prohibition and causing the growth of smuggling and secret tea drinking for Germans to get their fix of the black (or green or white) stuff! Even then, there were tea revolutionaries!

Holland's principal customer for tea in the 17th century was East Frisia, in Northwest Germany. They are massive tea drinkers—in fact, if East Frisia were a country in its own right, its annual tea consumption per capita would be the highest in the world, ahead of China and Ireland! When coffee became really popular throughout Europe and the rest of Germany in the 19th century, East

Left Tea chests, Hamburg, Germany.

HOW TO MAKE: A tea cloud

1 Make a strong brew of Assam tea.

2 Put a cube of sugar in a smallish cup or glass (the size of an espresso cup if you have one) and pour over some tea, being sure to leave room for the next layer of cream.

3 Now, pour the cream onto the back of a spoon resting on the edge of the cup so it sits as a layer on top—a little will mushroom downward into the tea and give you the "tea cloud."

4 Sip—you'll get a hit of the sugar and the cream helps to lighten this strong tea.

Who knew?

During the Second World War when tea was rationed in Germany, extra "teekarten" were distributed in the East Frisian region so that the heavy tea drinkers could get their daily tea quota.

Frisians stuck to tea because it was more economical—tea leaves could be used many times and there's no need for coffee grinders or filters. A little known fact to many is that Hamburg, the principal port in East Frisia, is a major player in the worldwide tea trade with numerous tea companies based there. In fact, Germany reexports more tea than it consumes; much of the premium teas consumed around the world have likely passed through one of Hamburg's tea importers.

The majority of tea drunk in Germany is loose leaf; there are over 2,500 specialist teashops across the country selling quality leaf teas from Darjeeling, Assam, Sri Lanka, and China. German tea drinkers are discerning and drink teas of a particularly high quality due in part to the high tax of over 4 Deutschmarks (1 US$) 2¼ pounds (1kg) applied to purchasing tea after the Second World War, regardless of the quality. This meant that better-quality teas proportionally became better value. Prior to the fall of the Berlin Wall, tea was subsidized in East Germany in part of a bartering arrangement. Postunification, the subsidy stopped and sadly tea consumption in this part of Germany has declined due to the hike in prices.

Back to East Frisia, in this neck of the woods there is a unique way of making and drinking tea (a kind of tea ceremony). Each cup of this special tea has three layers—the sugar (is the land), the tea (is the sea), and the cream (is the sky or cloud)—and there's no stirring allowed (see How to make a tea cloud, opposite).

Tea is so popular in East Frisia (or Ostfriesland, as the Germans know it) that there are two museums dedicated to tea that you can visit.

BÜNTING TEEMUSEUM
Brunnenstraße 33, 26789 Leer
www.buenting-teemuseum.de
In Lower East Frisia check out the tea museum in Leer where you can learn about the 400-year history of tea in this region and celebrate the local tea ceremony. Do as the locals do and say *prost tee*—cheers to tea!

OSTFRIESISCHES TEEMUSEUM
Am Markt 36, 26506 Norden
www.teemuseum.de
The second wonderful museum of tea lies in North East Frisia in Norden.

CHINESISCHES HAUS IM PARK SANSSOUCI
Am Grünen Gitter, 14469 Potsdam
www.spsg.de/schloesser-gaerten/objekt/chinesisches-haus
In complete contrast to the Vier Jahreszeiten Hotel, and rather unusual it has to be said, is the Chinese Tea-house Yu Garden in Potsdam—it's an exact copy of an original Chinese teahouse from Shanghai all adorned with gold but is situated in the beautiful setting of the Sanssouci Park. It was built back in the mid-18th century but still prompts open mouths today.

GRAB A TEA.
GERMANY

Take a stroll around this tranquil park followed by a stop at this perfect place for a cup of tea.

MEßMER MOMENTUM
Am Kaiserkai 10
20457 Hamburg
www.messmer.de/messmer-momentum
In the heart of the "tea district" of Hamburg is the Meßmer Momentum, another shrine to tea where you can browse exhibits, learn from experts, and enjoy a relaxed cup of tea from their extensive menu while relaxing in the comfortable tea lounge.

VIER JAHRESZEITEN HOTEL
Inner Alster lake
Neuer Jungfernstieg 9-14
D-20354 Hamburg
www.fairmont.com/vier-jahreszeiten-hamburg
And while you're in Hamburg, be sure to visit the very grand Vier Jahreszeiten Hotel—it is probably the best place to take an afternoon tea in its superluxurious and spectacular surroundings overlooking the lake.

Left and below Meßmer Momentum, Hamburg.

FRANCE

In France, the story of tea is similar to that in Great Britain, due to similar trade routes and the onset of globalization. But there is a significant difference. As in Britain, tea was introduced to France as a luxury and was enjoyed by aristocrats. In the 19th century, the Anglophile trend of "taking tea" spread across France and was soon enjoyed by anyone who was seen to be well off—soon there were more *salons de thé* in France than in England. But, it seems the French never took tea at home—it was enjoyed only by the wealthy or as a special event.

Nowadays, taking tea in France comes with all sorts of wondrous pastries, macarons, and tartes, and these smart spaces allow a welcome escape from the hustle and bustle of modern life. The French favor tea of the highest quality (no "ifs" or "buts" or "maybes"), with a delicate taste and they don't often take milk. What's more, there is a growing popularity for the terroirs of teas, as with wines, and for marrying teas with certain foods. And seeing as the French know a thing or two about both, it seems a tea revolution is happening already.

Tea in France has long been recognized for its medicinal properties—King Louis XIV was prescribed tea for his digestion and as a preventative against gout. The French, particularly in the Alpine regions and Provence, also have a great tradition for "tisanes" or herbal infusions with medicinal properties.

> **Great love affairs start with champagne and end with tisane.**
>
> Honoré de Balzac, *French novelist and playwright*

Opposite Handmade pitchers, cups, and mugs at the Astier de Villatte boutique along rue Saint-Honoré, Paris, France.

GRAB A TEA.
FRANCE

MARIAGE FRÈRES
13 rue des Grands-Augustins, 75006 Paris
www.mariagefreres.com
This historic French tea company has roots dating back to the 19th century when the company was formed in 1854 by the two brothers Henri and Edouard Mariage. There are various locations across France and worldwide selling a huge range of teas and tea paraphernalia. They also serve an extensive menu of tea and tea-related foods in a unique, tranquil, and refined setting. Sample the *douceurs du thé* (tea delights); our favorite iconic cake being the *carré d'or*—dark-chocolate sponge flavored with tea and salted caramel, decorated with edible gold leaf, and served with a red currant coulis.

LADURÉE
75 avenue des Champs-Elysées, 75008 Paris
www.laduree.com
If in Paris, another must-stop for eats and tea is Ladurée, famed since 1862 for its macarons. Various locations across Paris but we like their flagship *salon*.

DAME CAKES – SALON DE THÉ
70 rue Saint Romain, 76000 Rouen
www.damecakes.fr
The beautifully ornate doors give your welcome an awesome surrounding from the start. This *salon de thé* is a double-decker of a place but not with any hustle and bustle, no. Here is a quiet, almost serene atmosphere where the Mariage Frères teas and homemade delights, both sweet and savory, are there to transport you from the everyday humdrum. Head upstairs for the best view of the Notre Dame Cathedral. And if you can't get enough of the financiers or madeleines, then they have a takeout service.

CAMILI BOOKS & TEA
155 rue de la Carreterie, 84000 Avignon
www.camili-booksandtea.com
This tearoom is also a secondhand English bookshop. Step inside to find a table for tea and while away an hour while reading your new favorite book. Choose from a wide selection of teas and some top-notch cakes. During the summer months, head out to the gem of an outdoor patio for an alfresco iced tea. They also run English/French conversation groups every Friday—do you need to brush up on *votre français*?

THE VILLA EPHRUSSI DE ROTHSCHILD
06230 St.-Jean-Cap-Ferrat
www.villa-ephrussi.com
Just a 6-mile (10-km) drive from Nice or Monaco, make a detour to take tea in the icing-pink Villa Ephrussi de Rothschild. This exquisite Venetian villa has a tearoom with a view to die for—the Bay of Villefranche. Whether you want to sit and soak in the view while sipping on your tea or dash in for a quick pastry and a cup, you won't be disappointed. The gardens are jaw-droppingly beautiful, too.

AQUARELLE CAFÉ
16 Bis Avenue Alfred Borriglione, 06100 Nice
www.aquarelle-cafe.com
If you have a sweet tooth then check out this cupcake haven that does a good range of global teas. It's a bright and uplifting place with unusual and quirkily named cupcakes.

Eastern Europe, Russia, and Central Asia

As in Northern Europe (see pages 20–33), tea was also introduced to these regions in the 17th century but, in contrast to Northern Europe, tea arrived via land, specifically via the famous Silk Road caravans. The similarities of tea drinking in this region are the sharing of the tea-drinking moment and the process of making tea using a samovar.

EASTERN EUROPE

It seems that in the history of tea Eastern European countries were somewhat squeezed out, as strong tea cultures developed east in Russia through the Silk Road caravans and in Western Europe through the establishment of trading routes by sea. Tea arrived somewhat later in Eastern Europe. In fact, the Czech Republic it is said that tea didn't arrive until in 1848 when Mikhail Bakunin, the famous Russian anarchist, asked for tea in a Prague coffeehouse and was met by bewildered looks. Fortunately, Mikhail was also a mean tea maker and had bought some of his beloved tea with him, which he prepared for himself and the locals. Tea drinking took off with gusto and teahouses (or *cajovny*) sprung up throughout the city with over 150 trading at the outbreak of the First World War. Sadly, these died away during the Communist era; although there has more recently been a resurgence of *cajovny* where teas from around the world are drunk in a relaxed, convivial atmosphere.

Poland is a nation of big tea drinkers—ranking in the top 20 of tea consumers per capita in the world. Definitely more of a tea-drinking country than of coffee. There, tea is often offered black when being received as a guest in someone's house (don't forget to take off your shoes!). Milk versions of tea are called *bawarka*, which translates as Bavarian style. There is also a strong tradition of drinking fruit and herbal teas (what we'd strictly call tisanes, see page 134) as the ingredients for these grow plentifully and naturally in the countryside.

GRAB A TEA.
EASTERN EUROPE

CHADO
Uus tn 11, 10111 Tallinn
www.chado.ee
Estonia plays host to one of the most inviting-looking teashops in Eastern Europe; it's cozy, old-fashioned, and pretty much everything you'd expect from a teashop, nestled in the back streets of Tallinn. The quirky and friendly atmosphere leaves you completely at ease to browse through their collection of rare teas and learn all about the secrets of brewing a perfect cup. Be sure to strike up a conversation with the shop owner whose passion and love of tea can be felt almost instantaneously.

DOBRÁ ČAJOVNA
Václavské Náměstí 14, 11100 Prague
The Czech Republic tends to take a far more relaxed approach to tea, and throughout the country you can see even moreteahouses popping up. Dobrá Čajovna in the heart of Prague is often thought as helping ignite the new Czech tea revolution. Although there is now a chain of these teahouses across the nation and some could perceive it as being too touristy—we say, fear not! They offer a huge selection of specialist teas and have managed to create a beautiful ambience—we say, a thoroughly calming place to enjoy a wonderful cup of tea.

ČAJDŽINICA DŽIRLO
Kovači 16, 71102 Sarajevo
If it's rustic and utterly charming that you're after, then look no further! This effortlessly cool teahouse offers perfectly friendly and knowledgeable service while serving a great range of teas from around the world. If you're ever passing through Sarajevo (in the center of Bosnia and Herzegovina) be sure to pop in and experience this delightful place in all its glory. You'll undoubtedly spend hours drinking tea, swapping stories with other tourists, and engaging in meaningful discussions with the locals—what more could you possibly ask for from a local teahouse?

ČAJOVŇA V PODZEMÍ
Ventúrska 9, 811 01 Bratislava
Another hidden gem of a tearoom—and we mean hidden—is tucked away on a side street at the bottom of a discrete staircase in central Bratislava in Slovakia. Čajovňa V Podzemí offers a unique tea experience for those wanting to unwind. Here they offer a great mix of tea from around the world, in a laid-back and welcoming atmosphere. We've also heard great things about their hummus—and who doesn't love hummus? There definitely seems to be a trend developing—if it's a laid-back, friendly "hippy" atmosphere you're after, then it seems that Eastern Europe has it covered.

KAZAKSTAN AND UZBEKISTAN

Kazakstan was very much on the early trading routes between Asia and Russia and, as such, developed a strong tea-drinking culture. Tea is drunk by pretty much everyone, with and without food, often together in groups. Guests are always offered tea, which is poured from a large tea kettle into small, wide-mouthed saucers called *kasirs*. The *kasirs* are only ever half filled as the Kazaks have a fear of cold drinks, believing them to be bad for health. The tea is always drunk hot and when finished the *kasir* is passed back to be refilled. There is a constant movement within the room with tea being poured, passed around, passed back for refilling, and so on.

Uzbekistan sits smack bang in the middle of the Silk Road and has

paid hospitality to the travelers of the caravans for centuries. Central to this hospitality is the Uzbesk Tea Ceremony, a formal and graceful ritual. When a guest arrives, the host will serve tea, usually accompanied by a traditional snack of fresh flat, round bread. The freshly brewed tea is poured from a teapot into a ceramic cup known as a *piala* and then returned to the teapot three times, allowing the full flavor and aroma of the tea to develop. The first returning is called *loy*, the second *moy*, and only after the third time does it become *choy*, or tea. The fourth time, tea is poured into the guest's *piala*. As a token of respect for the guest, the host fills only one half of the *piala* and then, putting their left hand to their heart, with their right hand

holds out this *piala* to the guest. Tea, green or black, is always drunk hot to allow the full aroma and flavor to emerge. *Chaikhanas* (teahouses) are to be found everywhere in Uzbekistan and are usually crowded with men discussing business and the ways of the world over a porcelain pot of tea known as a *chianik*.

Above Drinking tea in a traditional teahouse on the Silk Road.

Opposite Exterior of a traditional teahouse in Prague's old town.

RUSSIA

As in many other countries, when tea was brought into Russia in the 17th century it was an aristocratic commodity. In stark contrast to its journey to other countries, though, tea from China traveled to Russia in caravans led by camels—a journey that took well over a year to complete. So, its status as a luxury item remained for quite some time.

But by 1880 the building of the Siberian railroad meant this journey time was cut drastically to just two months, making tea widely available and significantly cheaper. The samovar now came into its own. Samovar literally means "self-boiler" and this large urn, often made from copper, nickel, or silver, holds a significant amount of hot water and brews a superstrong tea, which is then diluted down to suit. Historically, the samovar was kept heated at all times to allow Russians to make tea whenever they like—perfect for the arrival of unexpected guests.

To this day, tea remains a staple in Russian life and is served after meals in an "afternoon tea" style—but, despite its moniker, this can take place at anytime of the day and in any place (home, office, park, car ...!). Tea is commonly served to visiting guests and becomes something of an event, with sweet and savory treats culminating in tea and cakes—even after an evening of some vodka. Some

Left An old samovar at a rural market.

HOW TO MAKE: A cup of Russian tea

Don't worry if you don't have a samovar on hand, you can experience all the flavors of a cup of Russian tea by following the steps below, though you will need a small teapot and a strainer.

1 To your teapot add 1 teaspoon of loose black tea (if you want the smoky Russian experience go for lapsang souchong) per person and add an extra one for the pot.

2 Pour a small amount of boiling water into the teapot.

3 Brew the tea for 3 to 4 minutes.

4 Pour a little of this concentrated tea into a cup and top off with hot water.

5 Pop in a slice of lemon (Russians rarely serve milk or cream in their tea) and plenty of sugar.

Who knew?

Would you like jam with your tea? Russians drink their tea without milk and often with a small side dish of what looks like jam. This fruit offering—called *varenye*—is eaten with a teaspoon while sipping the tea. The closest thing you might get to *varenye* is black currant jam —give it a try!

might even say that tea is more of the national drink than vodka.

While green and herbal teas are gaining in popularity, especially with younger tea drinkers, nearly all tea drunk in Russia is black, most of it coming from either China or India, with oolong and keemun teas from China being particularly popular.

If you like to take tea in Russian surroundings, then why not try the famous Russian Tea Room? It's not in Russia at all, but on the island of Manhattan, New York. It was founded by some of the members of the Russian Imperial Ballet in 1927 and still retains its modernist Russian-style décor. These days, it's renowned as an exclusive enclave of the New York intellectual and creative set.

> I say let the world go to hell, but I should always have my tea.
>
> Fyodor Dostoyevsky
> *Notes from Underground*

Who knew?

Where possible, Russians generally prefer to prepare loose tea and opt for a blend that has been smoked to varying degrees. The romantic notion is that the taste for smoked tea stems back to the days when it was transported by caravan, so would have been exposed to the smoke of the campfires along the route. But who knows ...?

Tea is a firm favorite among many Russian households, but where can it be enjoyed out and about in the streets of Russia? These go-to-places not only offer you the chance to revel in local hospitality but also serve up a pretty spectacular cup of tea!

DAGOMYS TEA PLANTATION
302 Zaporozhskaya St,
Uch-Dere, Sochi 354231
www.dagomystea.ru

For the hardcore tea fans out there, why not visit Dagomys Tea Plantation and explore the only place in Russia where tea is grown? There you can take a tour of the plantation, as well as enjoy tea in a wooden cabin, nestled within gorgeous natural surroundings. Tea is served from a traditional samovar and accompanied with local sweet treats and delicacies. If learning all about tea is not enough, there is also live folk music and women in full traditional costume—a must-see for those wanting an authentic Russian tea experience!

PERLOV TEA HOUSE
19 Myasnitskaya St, Moscow 101000

If you are on a walking tour of St. Petersburg, then you will most likely come across the Perlov teahouse—a great opportunity to mix learning about local history with a nice cup of tea! The building's elaborate façade is a celebration of Chinese architecture and stands in stark contrast to the more humdrum backdrop of the rest of Myasnitskaya St. Passersby stop to admire the intricate details of dragons and pagodas; but, it is what lies within that is truly worth a visit! Here, the beautiful Chinese design continues and the shop itself offers a vast array of high-end teas as well as coffee and many local candies.

GRAB A TEA.
RUSSIA

ASTORIA HOTEL
39 Bolshaya Morskaya,
St. Petersburg 190000
www.roccofortehotels.com/hotels-and-resorts/hotel-astoria

While Russia has its own established tea culture, if you're looking for a more typically British afternoon tea affair, then head on over to the Astoria Hotel's exclusive Rotunda lounge where they offer the city's "most exquisite afternoon tea"—that's quite the claim, but go and judge for yourself! Along with sipping fine tea from the hotel's specially designed porcelain, you can also indulge in freshly made sandwiches, cakes, pastries, and blinis! If there is ever a time to splurge, then what better way than with a gorgeous cup of sweet tea and slice of cake!

TRANS-SIBERIAN RAILWAY
www.trans-siberian.co.uk

Embarking on one of the epic Trans-Siberian Railway journeys is on many a bucket list. But what could make this journey even more enjoyable? You got it, a lovely cup of tea! Just imagine it, chugging along through Russia's vast landscape, staring out the window taking in spectacular scenery and meeting people from all walks of life. A romanticized image perhaps (let's not mention the six days in a metal train) but if you're after a truly social tea experience then this is it. Of course, you can buy tea and other goodies from the dining car, but it's good to know that each car of the train has its own samovar, which means you can bring your own tea—sit back and relax with your favorite blend. Perfect!

Middle East

The tea culture dominates in many Middle Eastern countries with centuries of history dating back to the ancient trading routes, most notably the Silk Road from China as well as routes from Sri Lanka and southern India. The importance of tea trading continues to this day with Dubai now playing the role of a major re-exporter of tea and an international doorway for the tea trade. Tea drunk in the Gulf is predominantly black tea, usually drunk with sugar and sometimes with added spices, especially cardamom. Whether or not you add milk to your brew will depend upon the customs of the local area.

TURKEY

Tea is huge in Turkey. Turkey is number one worldwide for per capita consumption and ranks number five for production. It's an integral part of everyday life—be it summer, winter, a big family gathering, or a quiet day at home. And it's not the touristy apple tea that Turkish people drink, it's a strong black tea; though they do also dip into the herbal arena with rosehip, sage, and linden blossom teas.

The origins of tea drinking in Turkey go back to the 16th century when the Silk Road caravans passed through the country. But the real explosion in tea drinking occurred in 1878 after the publication of *Çay Risalesi* (or *The Tea Pamphlet*), touting the health benefits of drinking tea by Mehmet Izzet, the then Governor of Adana. Although coffee was still the preferred hot drink during this period of history, tea consumption began to spread as teahouses opened in the Sultanahmet area of Istanbul. Also, tea became cheaper; four glasses of tea could be purchased for the price of just one cup of Turkish coffee.

The high consumption of tea is due to its widespread availability in teahouses and tea gardens all over the country, their role as hubs of social activity and the fact that Turkey has a well-established tea-producing region along its eastern Black Sea coast. Tea gardens, another social venue for drinking tea, gained popularity in the 1950s, especially in Istanbul, and were the place where families went for their social outings. As Turkish tea gardens are social hubs, expect to see kids running around, hear music playing, and plenty of lively conversation among young and old.

The tea—or should we say *çay*—is prepared as a strong concentrate and then diluted with hot water and sugar. Tea is prepared either in a samovar (see page 38) or in two separate pots. The lower pot boils the water, the smaller upper pot contains the tea leaves and is where the tea is infused to a strong liquor. This split of brewing allows each drinker to adjust the strength of tea exactly to their taste: strong, straight from the top pot, or in varying degrees of dilution by topping off with water from the bottom pot.

Tea is drunk from tulip-shaped glasses—nearly 400 million of these glasses are sold every year! The clear glass allows the drinker to appreciate the crimson color of the tea. Often two small sugar cubes are served with tea and in some towns in Eastern Turkey tea is taken in the *kitlama* style, where a cube of sugar is placed between the tongue and the cheek.

Turkish tea production began in the Black Sea town of Rize in the early 20th century. The government was instrumental in encouraging cultivation and production grew so much that some towns began to change their names to have the word *çay* (Turkish for tea) in them: the town of Mapavri became Çayeli and Kadahor became Çaykara (we like this idea of creating new town names with the word "tea" in). Today, the Çaykur state-controlled company produces over 60% of all Turkish tea production. Total tea production in Turkey is now enough to satisfy its domestic demand and have excess to export. The tea industry is an important economic player with over 200,000 families involved in the cultivation of tea either as owners of tea estates or employees in factories.

Who knew?

Tea culture in Turkey is strong and traditional. As a host you are supposed to serve tea for as long as your guests would like. You can never say you've run out of tea! If you're bargaining with a trader in the bazaar and have had your fill of tea, simply put your teaspoon on top of your glass the moment you finish your tea. This signals politely that you really have had enough tea, thank you.

HOW TO DRINK: Turkish tea

1 Make a really strong small pot of tea. Arrange glasses on a serving tray.

2 Fill the glasses a quarter full (half full produces an incredibly strong tea) and top off with water; add sugar to taste. Be sure to leave a ½-in (1-cm) gap at the top so that it's easy to drink without spilling or burning your fingers!

3 Hold the glass at the top with your thumb and index finger (there are no handles) and sip and enjoy!

Opposite Turkish men enjoying tea in a courtyard tea-house in a bazaar.

This page Drinking tea in Bab Makkah, Jeddah, Saudi Arabia.

Opposite Bags of tea in Qaysari Bazaar, Erbil Kurdistan, Iraq.

SAUDI ARABIA

Saudi Arabia is the second largest consumer of tea in this region with over 19 million cups of tea drunk daily. Drunk mostly black and imported mainly from Sri Lanka and Southern India (often via Dubai), tea is drunk in most social situations and always when business is being done. Glass cups are filled to the brim with hot tea, which may also be sweetened.

IRAQ

Tea in Iraq is prepared in a samovar (see page 38) or using the double-pot method (as in Turkey, see page 42). Generally the tea drunk in Iraq is particularly strong—it may be brewed for up to 15 minutes—and is served with at least a couple of spoons of sugar. Teahouses, called *chaixane*, are found all over Iraq and can range from a simple roadside stall with an urn to an elaborate establishment where men (rarely women) will gather to talk, play backgammon, smoke *nargile* (hookah pipes) and, of course, drink copious amounts of tea.

> **The Chinese say it's better to be deprived of food for three days than tea for one.**
>
> Khaled Hosseini
> *A Thousand Splendid Suns*

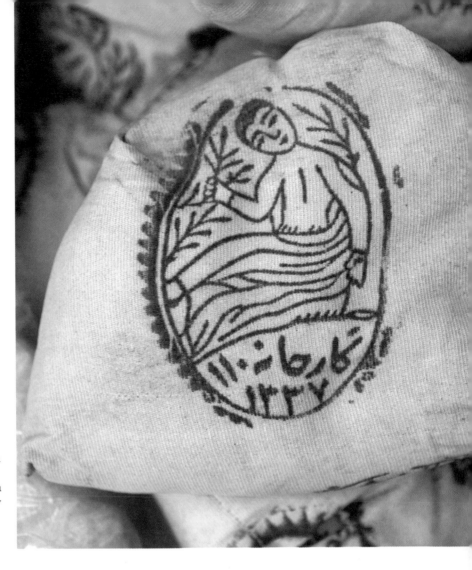

IRAN

Iranians not only drink an awful lot of tea, but they grow a massive amount of it, too. The fact that tea production exists at all in Iran can be traced back to the imagination and determination of an Iranian diplomat, Kashef Al Saltaneh. Around the end of the 19th century tea drinking in Iran was big business, the habit having been established because of the country's position on the Silk Road, but by now the British had a monopoly over the supply of tea from India. Spotting an opportunity, Kashef Al Saltaneh, a fluent French speaker, traveled to India posing as a French businessman. After learning all he could about the tea trade and growing tea, he smuggled some tea saplings back to Iran where he used all his experience to establish tea cultivation in the northern states of Gilan and Mazandaran. The tea bushes flourished and Iran is now the world's 7th largest producer of tea. Kashef Al Saltaneh is known today as the father of Iranian tea, and his mausoleum, in the city of Lahijan, houses a tea museum. It is also in this region that the best-quality Lahijan Spring tea is produced.

Despite producing its own tea, Iranians are such heavy tea drinkers that they also import much from Sri Lanka and India. Throughout the country the teahouses known as *chaikhanahs* serve tea in glass cups of varying strength. The tea is served strong from a samovar and may be diluted with additional hot water, depending upon the drinker's preference. Many Iranians like to sweeten their tea with sugar, particularly a native variety known as *kand*. Traditionally this rock sugar is held between the teeth and the tea is sipped through it.

Africa

As with the Middle East, North Africa has had a strong tea culture for centuries, with tea playing a very special role in society. An invitation to share a cup of tea is so much more than a polite drink with friends or strangers; it is an invitation into a home, into a family, and into their hearts. Tea is enjoyed anytime and anywhere—with breakfast, after meals, and anytime in between; at the local souks (markets), on the busy streets, or in the village square. In contrast, at the southern end of the continent the tea-drinking culture is all about rooibos, an indigenous plant that makes a refreshing infusion (see also page 134). The cultivation of tea is also important in Africa, with Kenya alone representing 22% of all world tea exports.

EGYPT

Tea, or *shai* as it is known in this neck of the woods, is very much the national drink of Egypt, being drunk by most of the population, young and old, rich and poor. Egypt imports most of its tea from Sri Lanka and Kenya, and the guaranteed supply of tea is so important that the government manages tea estates in Kenya.

There are two styles of tea drinking. In the northern part of the country it is called *koshary*, a fairly light tea that is usually sweetened with cane sugar and fresh mint leaves. In the south, *saiidi* is the most commonly drunk tea; this brew is a much stronger and more bitter version as the tea leaves are boiled vigorously over high heat for at least 5 minutes. The resultant dark, thick tea requires much sweetening.

Egyptians also have a passion for a native plant—hibiscus—and a caffeine-free herbal infusion of this plant is drunk both hot and over ice. This bright red, tart-tasting infusion is known as *karkady* and is often sweetened too.

MOROCCO, TUNISIA, AND ALGERIA

All three of these countries feature in the top 20 highest tea consumption per capita in the world (see page 18). The tea served in this region, often referred to as the Maghreb, is a brew of Chinese green tea (often Chunmee, a rather bitter green tea, see page 108) and North African nana mint.

Particularly important in Morocco where it is the national drink, this flavored tea (also sometimes called Touareg tea) serves almost a ceremonial purpose and is usually enjoyed with a hefty dose of sugar. Whether welcoming friends into your home, haggling at a souk, or having a roadside picnic, the preparation, serving, and drinking of mint tea as a refreshment is a ritual and an art form—you could say, it's a prerequisite for almost any social interaction.

Making and serving tea in Morocco is a mini ceremony in its own right. In contrast to Turkey where women mostly prepare and serve tea, it's the men in Morocco who hold center stage in the tea-making ritual. And it's impolite to refuse it.

Once the mint tea is brewed, it is poured from a height both to create a frothy top and to cool it down. The tea is drunk in colorful, ornately patterned small glasses that are common to the region. Mint tea preparation varies from region to region; it is sweeter in the north of Morocco than in the south, and in differing parts of the country, wormwood leaves, pine nuts, or lemon verbena may be added.

HOW TO MAKE: Moroccan mint tea

As with all countries, there are significant regional variations, but here's our basic mint tea recipe:

1 Arrange some small tea glasses on a tray.

2 Mix some Chinese green tea with fresh or dried mint leaves and a large cube of sugar (or at least 2 teaspoons) in a metal or stainless-steel teapot (or whatever you can find).

3 Pour hot water into the pot and let the tea infuse for several minutes.

4 Pour the tea from a height (about 12 inches/30cm; this might take a bit of practice as you don't want any nasty accidents) into the small glasses, to create a frothy brew. Garnish with fresh mint leaves and breathe in deeply as the mint aroma fills the room.

Though we call this style of tea Moroccan here, it is also referred to as Maghrebi tea and is drunk throughout the region in northwest Africa in the countries of Morocco, Tunisia, Algeria, Libya, and Mauritania.

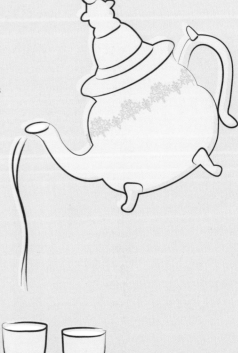

This page Mint tea lined up on a market stall in the Jemaa El Fna market, Marrakech, Morocco.

KENYA

Kenya is not only the world's third largest tea producer but also the number one exporter of tea. Tea is one of Kenya's main exports. Tea was first planted here in 1904 from seedlings taken from northern India by British planters. The climate in Kenya, with its rainfall and warm temperatures, is ideal for year-round cultivation of tea. Most of the tea produced is black (see pages 120 and 132) and continues to be exported to Britain where it's used for tea bags. Some 60% of all tea production in Kenya is from small holders rather than large company estates. The city of Mombasa hosts one of the world's major tea auctions and also serves as the main port for exports of tea not just from Kenya but also from the nearby landlocked countries of Rwanda and Malawi.

Tea drinking in Kenya follows a mixture of styles—it embraces the traditional "tea time" of the British colonial past but serves a tea borrowed from India: a milky, spicy, sweet chai tea.

Above Tea harvest in Kachege, Kenya.

Right Bags upon bags of raw rooibos await processing.

SOUTH AFRICA

It seems like everyone has their own way of saying the popular tea drink in this region of the world, but we like to pronounce rooibos as "roy-boss"; some people don't worry about trying to say it any which way and just call it redbush tea instead. So, feel free to choose the way to say it that suits you.

Botanically speaking, rooibos is not a true tea (see pages 90 and 134): it's strictly a herb that grows as a small shrubby bush, its species name is *Aspalathus linearis* and it grows in just one place—the Cederberg region of South Africa, near Cape Town. The ultraclean air swirling around the steep mountains provides the perfect environment for the rooibos plant. Efforts have been made to grow rooibos outside of the Cederberg region but none has been successful.

More than 300 years ago, the original bushmen of the Cederberg area—the Khoi and San peoples—discovered rooibos. Back in their day, they bashed the leaves, piled them in heaps allowing them to ferment then spread them out in the sun to dry. Then, they brewed the leaves in hot water over a fire. And that's pretty much what the commercial rooibos production is like today. The drying out of the rooibos under the African sun changes the color of the leaves to a deep mahogany.

The green needlelike leaves of the rooibos plant are naturally caffeine-free. Along with the beautiful coppery color of the rooibos infusion and the natural nutty and full-bodied flavor, this tea is fast becoming sought after as a great caffeine-free alternative to black teas. Traditionally, rooibos is enjoyed with lemon and sugar or honey, but as tea culture is growing (and experimenting) it's also being served as espressos, iced teas, and lattes.

South Asia and South East Asia

No other region in the world can boast such tea credentials, from the birthplace of tea, to colonial wars; from major tea-producing nations (four of the world's top six are in this region, see also pages 16 and 18) to tea ceremonies a plenty. Tea can be found on virtually every street corner and is central to many of the nations' social, political, and economic histories. The way tea is prepared and drunk is, however, as varied in styles as the rich history and culture of the region itself.

INDIA

Tea only became a national beverage in India during the 19th century, after the British began to create large-scale tea plantations to satisfy their country's growing thirst. Even though it's one of the world's biggest suppliers of tea, this relatively recent conversion means that India has not yet had time to develop the long-standing rituals or ceremonies such as those found in China and Japan.

That said, they do drink their tea—*cha-ya* or *chai*—in a certain way, and they really love to drink tea. Most often, chai is a thick, strong black tea that is spiced with cardamom, fennel seeds, ginger, cloves, and other spices, sweetened and boiled in milk. Everyone has their own favorite recipes that are passed down from generation to generation. Pretty much every street will have its chai wallah, a street vendor who will serve passersby with his own special brew alongside savory snacks, such as samosas.

Chai has now become a popular beverage in the Western world. No self-respecting coffee bar would be complete without an offering of chai or chai latte as they are often called. Nothing can really beat the authentic homemade version of chai, but sadly, because of the time involved in preparation those served in Western coffee shops are often sugary, powdered inferior versions of this Indian classic or are simply plain tea "spiced up" with the addition of a liquid concentrate. Not so nice, after all.

 **Who knew?**

Chai vendors serve their wares in small clay pots, which are smashed on the floor after each use—well, it certainly saves on cleaning them! Clay pot wallahs can throw a clay pot for chai in 8 seconds flat! They are half-baked and biodegradable —the monsoon rains and baking hot sun soon cause the pots to disintegrate into the soil.

Opposite, clockwise from top left Child enjoying chai in Haridwar; a chai wallah pouring tea in Mysore; tea and spices for chai preparation; chai seller with glasses of chai; chai on a stove; and a chai wallah in Tiruchirappalli.

HOW TO MAKE: Chai

It may seem strange for hipsters used to ordering chai in some fancy coffeehouse that this is how tea has been prepared and drunk in southern Asia since the 19th century. There are probably as many recipes for chai in India as there are people, using various permutations of tea, spices, water, milk, and sugar. The basic steps for making a traditional chai would be:

1 Prepare a spicy masala mixture; this could contain any of the following: cardamom pods, cloves, cinnamon sticks, ginger root, black peppercorns, and nutmeg. Ideally grind down to a fine powder; though, some people prefer to keep the spices whole.

2 Tip the masala mix into a saucepan of water (say about 2 cups (500ml) along with some strong black tea leaves.

3 Bring to a boil and keep boiling for 5 minutes.

4 Add 2 cups (500ml) of milk, bring back to a boil, and boil for at least another 5 minutes.

5 Add sugar (jaggery or palm sugar is popular) to taste.

The water to milk ratio, amount and type of spices used, amount of sugar, length of boil; all these are variable and different combinations will deliver different flavors. Experiment to find what suits you best.

6 Then, strain the contents of the pan so that the tea leaves and any whole spices are removed.

7 Serve and enjoy.

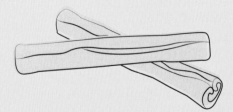

SRI LANKA

To give it its full name, the Democratic Socialist Republic of Sri Lanka (or Ceylon as it was known before 1972) was introduced to both tea cultivation and tea drinking by the British colonials. To this day there continues a tradition of drinking tea, specifically "milk tea," which is served throughout the day, except in the middle of the morning when tea is drunk without the white stuff (milk).

On this island in the Indian Ocean, tea is often sweetened with a smattering of jaggery: a form of concentrated crystalline sweetener, sold in little blocks, often made from sugar cane juice or the sap of date palms.

 **Who knew?**
When the tea is poured from a great height (about a yard in old measures; that's 90cm in metric), it's referred to as *yaara they* or "yard tea"; this skillful pouring procedure ensures a very bubbly consistency to the finished tea.

PAKISTAN

Surprisingly, Pakistan doesn't produce tea but consumes a lot, being the world's third biggest importer with most tea coming from Kenya. Again, tea here is drunk with milk. *Elaichi chai*, a milky tea with cardamom, is drunk throughout Pakistan but is particularly popular in Karachi. *Doohd pati* is a milk tea in the purest form, a very thick milky tea with no water added at all and is popular in the Punjab. In the northern Khyber Pakhtunkhwa region, the tea of choice tends to be a green tea known as *kahwah*, while in Kashmir they drink a green tea chai with pistachios and cardamom, which turns a shade of pink during making.

Who knew?

A famous Balti proverb states that the first time you take tea with someone you are a stranger, the second time you become an honored guest, the third time you become family.

Below Tea pluckers at Haputale tea plantation in the highlands of Sri Lanka.

THAILAND

Would you buy tea in a plastic bag? Well, in Bangkok no one even bats an eye if you're walking down the street with a plastic bag of tea, with plenty of ice cubes inside. With its bright amber color, Thai iced tea is the perfect drink on a sticky hot day—and you get a fair few of those in this region of the world.

This version of milky tea can be found throughout Asia. It's usually served over ice and its ingredients consist of strongly brewed black tea, sweetened condensed milk, evaporated milk, and various aromatic spices, including star anise, green cardamom, orange blossoms, cloves, cinnamon, and ground tamarind. The overbearing sweetness of this tea binds all the flavors together. Thai iced tea is the perfect complement to spicy cuisine.

MYANMAR

Myanmar is one of the few countries in the world where tea is eaten as well as drunk. Yes, you read that right. Eaten. *Lahpet* is Burmese for fermented or pickled tea; it's something of a national delicacy and historically was exchanged as a peace offering between warring kingdoms and, in fact, is still offered and eaten when settling disputes. There is even a saying that demonstrates the importance of *lahpet*: "Of all the fruit, the mango's the best; of all the meat, pork's the best; of all the leaves, *lahpet*'s the best."

In Myanmar, *lahpet* is traditionally made by taking the best fresh tea leaves, steaming them for about 5 minutes before either drying or fermenting them. The young steamed leaves are then heaped together into a pulp and placed into bamboo baskets, which are then placed in pits and pressed down by heavy weights. The baskets are checked from time to time to see how everything is progressing and sometimes the leaves are resteamed. Pickled tea can be bought in packages throughout Myanmar (and is also available online for those adventurous types).

The pickled tea has a slightly sweet and sour taste and leafy texture; some pickled teas are flavored with spices such as ginger. Probably the most popular use of this tea is in pickled tea salad or *lahpet thohk*, a favorite national dish, to be accompanied, of course, by a cup of refreshing green tea.

HOW TO: Pickle tea

Pickling tea in the traditional manner may prove a little difficult and time consuming, but this quicker method delivers a pretty good version. Give it a try.

1 Place 1 cup (250ml) vinegar, ¾oz (20g) green tea leaves (Sencha), and 1 cup (250ml) water in a pan over medium heat.

2 Bring to a boil then reduce the heat to medium–low and simmer for 30 minutes.

3 Drain, rinse, and discard any hard pieces. Squeeze out the excess liquid.

4 Blend with 5½ tablespoons sesame oil, 4 tablespoons peanut oil, 1 tablespoon fish sauce, and 2 chopped garlic cloves. Stir in 2 tablespoons lemon juice.

Your pickled tea can be kept in the refrigerator for up to 3 months.

VIETNAM

Vietnam is the world's 6th largest tea producer and its tea-drinking culture goes back thousands of years. Tea drinking is an integral part of Vietnamese culture. Present everywhere from holidays to weddings, tea brings friends and family together in conversation and celebration. Most tea drunk in Vietnam is plain green tea but it can also be combined with herbal remedies or scented with flowers.

Lotus tea is popular during Tet, the Vietnamese Lunar New Year, a unique tea made in a traditional way. An ancient Hanoi people, known as Tràng An, were renowned for their skills in making and drinking lotus tea. In Vietnam, the lotus flower is seen as pure and serene and a bloom that is said to "gather the essence of heaven and earth in its scent."

To have the finest lotus tea, lotus flowers must be picked when they have just bloomed and kept fresh. It is believed that the best lotus flowers—because their blooms are larger and more fragrant—are collected from certain locations, such as Tinh Tam Lake in Hue City and the ponds of Quăng Bá village near West Lake in Hanoi. Once the blossoms are picked, the lotus flower buds are very carefully peeled back, the petals preserved without a single rip or tear and then it's combined with the fresh green tea. After all the buds are full and rebuilt they are put aside overnight, and the next evening the process is reversed and the now wonderfully aromatic lotus tea is extracted.

CAMBODIA

Tea is popular throughout Cambodia and has significance for certain rites of passage. For instance, tea plays a particularly important role in wedding ceremonies when the bride and groom offer a ritual cup of tea to their ancestors. This ceremony calls for those who have passed away, both for family members and for friends, to offer their blessings and observe the wedding, if not in body, but in spirit. It is a time to reflect on those close to the wedding party and to include them in the joyful day.

Above Lucky Seven, a famous and popular teashop in Yangon, Myanmar.

CHINA

It's no surprise that, as tea was allegedly discovered in China by the Emperor Shen Nung in 2737BC, China today produces more tea than any other nation in the world—over a whopping 1.6 million tons a year, most of it is consumed within China, with only 18% being exported of which just 1% goes to Europe. Tea was traditionally considered to be one of the seven daily necessities and so, naturally, everyone drank tea. And, as we all know, there are an awful lot of people in China.

In the tea world, China is unique —it's the only country in the world to produce all six styles of tea, predominantly green but also black, oolong, yellow, white, and pu-erh (see also pages 104–133). There are centuries of history relating to how tea should be cultivated, processed, served, and consumed, and so the Chinese really do know a thing or two about tea. And it rubs off, the Chinese name for tea—*chá*—has traveled to all corners of the globe.

There are literally thousands of teahouses across China and many customs associated with tea drinking. Many family gatherings take place in teahouses where extended families will get together especially on Sundays and for special festivals.

Traditionally, serving tea was a mark of respect to someone of a higher rank. Today, it is still served as something special, often at a wedding where it is served by the bride and groom to their parents to express gratitude and as a symbol of acceptance into the extended families of both parties. The bride and groom will kneel in front of their parents and offer tea to express their thanks

for bringing them up and making them who they are. The parents will respond by handing the bride and groom a red envelope, which symbolizes good luck.

While there are many formal ceremonies associated with drinking tea in China, most people drink their tea from glass jars that they carry with them during the day. The jars will contain tea leaves and will be regularly topped off with hot water. So the concept of "tea-on-the-go" has been popular in China for years.

Below Enjoying tea in a teahouse at the ancient Lizhou township in Xichang, Sichuan province.

WANGYE TEMPLE
Fuxi Riverside, Ziliujing District, Zigong 643000

What better way to enjoy tea than in a 100-year-old temple turned teahouse? Located above the Fuxi River in Zigong, this is the perfect place to come and explore one of the most beautiful Sichuan teahouses. Displaying untouched ancient architecture as well as gorgeous scenery, Wangye Temple offers a flawless backdrop to relax and enjoy fine tea. Here you can spend your time socializing and feel like a true local, or if you'd prefer you can simply sit back and take in the peaceful surroundings. While many people travel to Zigong to learn about the town's salt-mining history or visit the famed dinosaur museum, the spectacular teahouses that the region has to offer are definitely the star attraction in our eyes.

LAO SHE TEAHOUSE
Building 3, Zhengyang Market, Qianmen West Street, Xicheng District, Beijing 100051
www.laosheteahouse.net

Undoubtedly one of the more famous teahouses in Beijing, Lao She Teahouse offers a unique tea experience that aims to transport you back to the days of Old Beijing. Here you can enjoy Chinese tea and snacks with a side helping of Chinese theater! Each night features a 90-minute show offering the best of Chinese traditional arts, ranging from acrobats and comedy to Peking Opera. Although considered pretty touristy nowadays, the place definitely still has its charm and you will find it full of locals who come to enjoy the entertainment. If you're looking for somewhere to have a fun-filled night and soak up authentic Beijing culture with tea on tap, then this is the place!

MALIANDAO, AKA TEA STREET
Maliandao Street, Beijing 100055

If you've got a spare afternoon (or even a whole day) and wandering around teashops and markets is your idea of heaven, then definitely check out Maliandao Street in Beijing. Its other name is Tea Street and as soon as you arrive, you'll see why. Experts and novices alike can rejoice in the abundance of tea on offer and purchase any type of tea paraphernalia. Spend hours on the hunt for the perfect tea—each seller will be more than happy to let you try before you buy and will help you find exactly what you're after. The language barrier has the potential to be a slight issue, so have a few key phrases up your sleeve but, if in doubt, we always find nodding and pointing always works a charm.

MOUNT HUASHAN TEAHOUSE
Huayin 714200

Daredevils who like to unwind with a brew can probably be found atop Mount Huashan—widely classed as one of the most petrifying mountain trails in existence. At one point the only way to continue your journey is via tiny planks that have been literally bolted to the mountainside; seriously, look it up—the pictures are enough to make us feel woozy. However, amazingly located at the southern peak of this death-defying trek is a Taoist temple that now acts primarily as a teahouse! Taking tea at an altitude of over 7,087 feet (2,16 m) is surely a once-in-a-lifetime opportunity, and a must for the braver tea fans out there. They serve an insanely strong black tea to accompany the breathtaking views and this cup should be enough to get your adrenaline levels back to normal—if you make it to the top, that is.

HEMING TEAHOUSE
12 Shaocheng Road, Qingyang District, Chengdu 610015

If, like us, you love a spot for people watching then this teahouse will be right up your street. In Chengdu's central People's Park—a great space for some ambling away from the hustle and bustle—head on over to the Heming Teahouse; here is a beautifully tranquil spot to relax and watch the world go by. You'll find locals playing cards as well as tourists relaxing by the lake, enjoying the scenery. Many of the larger parks in China have numerous teahouses hidden within them—we recommend putting on your comfiest shoes and spending the day exploring the local parks to see what hidden gems, and what teas, you can discover!

GRAB A TEA.
CHINA

SONG FANG MAISON DE THÉ
227 Yongjia Road, Shanghai 200031
www.songfangtea.com

This specialist teashop in Shanghai serves up premium Chinese teas as well as offering a lovely selection of blended teas from France. The founder is a French native who has channeled her love of tea into a business celebrating the best of both Chinese and French culture. Split across a charming three-story house, Song Fang offers the best of both worlds with a traditional shop on the first floor as well as a modern and welcoming teahouse on the upper level. The staff are knowledgeable (they sell 70 types of tea) and friendly, and the change in pace upon entering the building can be felt instantly—definitely worth popping in to escape the busy streets of Shanghai and taste some truly exceptional tea!

Below Canisters of tea at Song Fan Maison de Thé, Shanghai.

CHINESE TEA CEREMONY

Where to begin with the Chinese tea ceremony, or what is also known as *gong fu cha* ceremony? *Gong fu* translates as "the time for tea" or "making tea with effort," which references the time and effort it takes to make tea traditionally.

As you'd expect for a country that has centuries of tea experience and an absolutely massive landmass, China does indeed have ceremonies to honor tea dating back to the early 17th century. *Gong fu* does indeed sound like *kung fu* (see below) but there really is no place for Bruce Lee antics here.

Let's start with some simple facts:
- China is a big country with a massive population.
- The Chinese have drunk tea for centuries.
- They drink a lot of tea.
- They treat it with the utmost respect.

All of the above means that if we were to refer to a single definitive Chinese tea ceremony we'd be way off the mark. Quite simply, there are many different versions.

What is a common thread, however, is that all ceremonies are performed with a sense of artistry and in an environment of calm serenity. The teapot and cups are usually made from clay with varying degrees of ornateness. What is also very true is that "making tea with effort" is certainly the best way to sum up a preparation method that to those who brew their tea for 30 seconds with a paper tea bag would see as Herculean. What follows below, for the sake of brevity, is what we see as some of the ceremony's common features.

The ceremony

1 The ceremony begins with the teapot being warmed with boiling water. Next, the tea leaves are added to the pot, usually with a bamboo scoop.

2 Then, hot—but not boiling—water is added to rinse the leaves; this water is then discarded. When the leaves are rinsed like this, the maker of the tea gets the first aromas of the tea being made.

3 More hot water is poured in; again, not boiling water as tea leaves are sensitive to temperature. The teapot is intentionally filled to overflowing. Any debris or bubbles that form on the surface are then scooped away gently to keep the tea from around the mouth of the teapot, which is then closed with the lid.

4 Hot water (often the same water that was discarded in step 3) is poured over the outside of the teapot to keep the pot warm all over. The tea within is allowed to infuse for a period of time, often as short as 1 minute, before being poured in a continuous motion into cups that are arranged in a semicircle. The cups are only half-filled, the empty half signifies friendship and affection.

5 The tea is then passed to those drinking it, who will first breathe in the aroma before drinking in three swallows.

Who knew?
You might think that *gong fu* sounds a bit like *kung fu* and you'd be right. In fact, the Chinese symbols for *gong fu* are the same as for these martial arts.

The art of making and preparing tea is known as cha dao. In this day and age, it may appear to be a time-consuming method, but its symbolism and ritualism demonstrates the important role that tea still plays in Chinese culture.

TAIWAN

Taiwan is famous both for its production of oolong tea (see page 116) and, more recently, for a new phenomenon known as bubble tea.

Pearl milk tea, boba milk tea or, as most of us know it, bubble milk tea started out in the 1980s in Taiwan, and its popularity has spread throughout Asia where it's usually sold by street vendors. It has a bit of a cult following in the West, too—with funky bubble tea bars opening up in smart city locations across North America, Europe, and the Middle East. This contemporary counterpart to Chinese tea is a mixture of tea, powdered milk, flavorings, sugar syrup, and black tapioca balls or "bubbles." Bubble tea joins the global trend for sweeter forms of tea or for using traditional tea leaves in modern and exciting new ways.

TIBET

Tibet is host to perhaps one of the most obscure tea traditions. Strong black tea leaves or pu-erh are simmered overnight to create a superstrong tea concentrate. This is then churned with yak or goat milk butter and salt to create a thick, frothy drink. Far from unusual for Tibetans, this is drunk by most people at least once a day as its warming properties and high calorie content form a key source of nutrition.

 **Who knew?**
Bubble milk tea might contain tea but it also contains lots of other ingredients—calorie-wise, one cup can add up to a lot more than your average hamburger!

Above Refreshing bubble tea or boba.

Opposite A Ngakpa, a Tibetan yogi, drinking a butter tea in Namzong, Qinghai province.

JAPAN

Japan is probably the country best known in the world for the ceremonial aspect of drinking tea. Over the centuries the Japanese have made the preparation and drinking of tea a revered art form. The principles of the Japanese tea ceremony—or *Cha-no-yu*—are rooted in the humility and respect of those involved, the appreciation of the moment's uniqueness and the art of simplicity and balance.

Green tea is by far the most popular beverage in Japan. It is so widely available that the Japanese simply refer to it as "tea" or "o-cha." This term can refer to a variety of green teas, depending on the growing conditions of the tea bush it came from, where on the plant the leaves were plucked, how they were steamed, dried, and processed and for how long for. Over the course of hundreds of years, the Japanese have developed many green teas that are an inherent part of their culture and everyday life (see page 110).

THE STORY BEHIND IT

Tea was first introduced to Japan by Buddhist monks who had traveled to China in the 700s, but for many years it was only consumed among those in religious and royal circles. It wasn't until 1191 when a Japanese priest named Eisia returned from a long stint in China that the cultivation and consumption of tea became widespread. He had traveled to China to study Zen Buddhist meditation and had been introduced to the Chinese custom of making tea from powdered leaves, therefore consuming the whole leaf. He proclaimed that Matcha, meaning "fine powder tea," played a crucial role in Zen meditation as it helped keep tiredness at bay. He went on to write Japan's first tea specialty book highlighting the health benefits of drinking Matcha (see what we love about this tea, too, on page 112).

Matcha soon became available to those who could afford it; a luxury item for the aristocracy and ruling samurai-warrior elite. If the rest of society wanted a taste, they had to come up with other ways to make it more affordable—and that's just what they did.

Genmaicha is green tea mixed with toasted rice. The poorest in Japanese society would often find themselves without food for long periods, so they added rice to the tea to act as a filler. This extra ingredient reduced the amount of tea needed and therefore its cost. The story goes that a man in Kyoto came across this concoction by accident, when he dropped a piece of his mochi (rice cake) into his cup of tea, and didn't want it to go to waste. Today, genmaicha is drunk by everyone and is also known as "popcorn tea" due to the popped rice resembling popped corn.

The majority of green tea drunk today in Japan is Sencha, a tea developed during the 18th century. It requires plucking the youngest tea leaves from the bush and then steaming and crumpling them as they are dried to prevent fermentation (see also page 100). Gyokuro is considered a higher-quality version of Sencha, because the leaves have been grown under shade, rather than being exposed to sunlight. (For more on Japanese green tea, see page 110.)

TEA DRINKING IN 21ST-CENTURY JAPAN

Step onto any street, into any café, office block, or inside any home in Japan and you can be sure tea will make an appearance. Hot or cold, tea is often provided free of charge

HOW TO MAKE: Matcha tea, the traditional way

The traditional way to drink Matcha is whisked into hot water using a bamboo whisk and served in a bowl. This makes a deliciously smooth and frothy tea. Genuine Matcha has a natural sweetness to it; it won't taste bitter or harsh, like some green teas do. It tastes rich, smooth, and has a natural, fresh, lasting green tea flavor.

1 Add a scoop of Matcha to your bowl (that's about ½ teaspoon).

2 Add a small amount of warm water—not too hot or you'll burn the leaves.

3 Give it a whisk—you can use a traditional bamboo whisk, as the Japanese do, if you like, but an electric handheld whisk works like a charm.

4 Top off with warm water. Enjoy and feel serene.

Because Matcha is a powder, there are lots of ways to drink and eat it. See pages 112, 168, 173, 179, 180, 192, 196, 199, and 200.

in restaurants and sold in bottles or cans in vending machines, kiosks, and grocery stores. Western-style black tea (or *kocha*) sometimes sweetened with milk and sugar in chilled bottles, is available, but green tea is the staple in Japanese tea-drinking habits, with oolong growing in popularity.

Within the home, green tea is consumed morning, noon, and night, and is always offered to guests as a sign of hospitality. This will almost certainly be loose-leaf tea put through a strainer and prepared for you with care by the host. Ask for sugar, and you'll definitely reveal yourself as a *gaijin* or "foreigner." Sugar is not added to green teas, as it is considered a great palate cleanser, and many Japanese people drink green tea instead of water to stay hydrated. This trend has contributed to the rise in green tea "on the go"—ready-to-drink bottled green teas, which are widely available for the busy lifestyles of today's tea drinkers.

The younger generation are aware of other drinks, such as grape-, melon-, and peach-flavored fizzy sodas, that compete for space in stores and vending machines. As of yet, though, green tea remains unchallenged—with old and young alike continuing to opt for green tea as their beverage of choice. It makes sense; there aren't many drinks out there that can top green tea on taste, refreshment, and health benefits combined.

HOTEL CHINZANSO
10-8, Sekiguchi 2-chome, Bunkyo-ku, Tokyo 112-8680
www.hotel-chinzanso-tokyo.com
You could be forgiven for thinking you'd fallen down a rabbit hole and landed in an enchanted forest when paying a visit to Hotel Chinzanso. Before entering you're in the heart of the relentless hustle and bustle of Tokyo and then once inside you're met with a vast and elegant entrance area, and a floor-to-ceiling glass window looking out onto the hotel's stunning garden. A hotel and outdoor private garden as spacious as these are hard to come by in Tokyo. Known as an "urban oasis," the hotel's garden is in bloom throughout the year, and it is within this haven that the hotel's traditional teahouses can be found. The hotel has a resident "tea master" who can lead the tea ceremony, and we can personally recommend this to be an informative yet immersive experience. The hotel also offers the largest spa facility in Tokyo, including an all-weather swimming pool and natural hot springs.

TONDAYA
Ichijo-agaru Omiya Kamigyo-ku Kyoto 602-8226
www.tondaya.co.jp
Tondaya is a lifestyle museum that offers a set menu of activities including a tea ceremony and kimono dressing. For a reasonable rate you can also have a tour of the building and a bento box lunch. To soothe the creative types they also offer calligraphy and origami classes. And for a bit of fun you can take a step back in time and imagine yourself as a member of the royal court, playing a couple rounds of some "ancient imperial Japanese games." The Machiya, a traditional wooden townhouse, was originally built in 1885 and used as a kimono wholesaler with a workshop in the front, and it's located about a 25-minute bus ride from Kyoto station.

GRAB A TEA.
JAPANESE TEA CEREMONIES

JOUKEIAN
Sannai cho 1-24 Sennyuji Higashiyamaku, Kyoto
www.joukeian.gotohp.jp
Joukeian is a short drive from Kyoto station and is run by Matsumoto Soko who has over 25 years experience in practicing the art of the tea ceremony. She offers a selection of courses ranging from short to full (what's known as *chaji*) and even offers a night course where you can experience the ceremony by candlelight.

Below A teahouse and view of the garden at the Hotel Chinzanso, Tokyo.

JAPANESE TEA CEREMONY

Maybe the most talked about tea ceremony around the world, the Japanese tea ceremony is known as *Cha-no-yu*, which roughly translates as "hot water for tea." That sounds so simple doesn't it? Thankfully, from a tea lover's perspective, it is anything but.

The tea ceremony centers on the preparation and serving of Matcha in the presence of guests, and a full-length ceremony can last about four hours. Each act involved is designed to focus the senses on the task at hand, and distractions are kept to a minimum.

It is known for being a very peaceful experience and yet its origins lie among the rowdy gatherings of the rich who took great pleasure in acquiring precious tea-making utensils and proudly displaying them in their grand halls.

By the 15th century, Zen Buddhist masters had their own ideas on serving tea to guests. Their methods had a more spiritual motivation—moving away from valuing material possessions and more toward appreciating simple beauty within themselves and in their surroundings, which became the basis of the tea ceremony.

It wasn't until the end of the 19th century, when the warrior-samurai class was abolished, that women took over from men as the main practitioners of tea. From this point on a young lady was required to study the tea ceremony in order to develop fine manners and grace. Below we outline the key steps carried out at a Japanese tea ceremony.

The ceremony

1 The guest is greeted by the host with a bow at the entrance gate.

2 The guest washes their hands in a stone washbasin and they also remove their shoes before entering the teahouse. This last bit is common practice in all Japanese homes and traditional buildings.

3 At a full-length ceremony a small meal will be served; however, in shorter versions a little sweet treat will be offered at the start of the ceremony.

4 The tea urn, scoop, and bowl are wiped down in a symbolic gesture of purifying the utensils about to be used.

5 Using the scoop, the host transfers the Matcha into the bowl and then adds hot water from a kettle using a bamboo ladle. The mixture is then mixed with a bamboo whisk.

6 The guest(s) is then offered the freshly made Matcha tea and it is placed in front of them. The guest should graciously thank their host with a slight bow of the head.

7 The bowl should be placed in the left hand and guided to the lips with the right. If there is more than one guest, then the first guest wipes the area he/she has just drunk from and passes the bowl to the next guest, who will drink from the same place as the first guest; this gesture is supposed to symbolize the bonding of all participants.

8 Conversation throughout will usually be limited to talk of the utensils and the decorations within the teahouse.

The tea used in the ceremony is Matcha, a very fine powder of ground-shade-grown green tea leaves (more on this on page 112). To prepare the Matcha tea, a few simple utensils are required:
• a bowl (*chawan*)
• a bamboo whisk (*chasen*)
• a bamboo tea scoop (*chashaku*)
• a sifter (*furui*)
• a bamboo ladle (*hishaku*)
• a large kettle (*kama*)
• a hearth or heat source.

The Americas and Australasia

There's something of a revolution going on in the world of tea in North America. More than 300 years after tea played a role in the original American Revolution, tea is undergoing a major facelift as tea drinkers are discovering quality teas from around the world served in even more locations and even more styles: hot, iced, blended with all sorts of other ingredients, and shaken and stirred. When Starbucks acquired Teavana, a major chain of teashops, in late 2012 it was apparent something was really stirring in the world of tea. And downunder, it's a story of pioneers, cosmopolitan tea culture, and the "make a brew wherever you are in the bush" device.

USA

The United States is famed for three things teawise: the Boston Tea Party, its huge consumption of iced rather than hot tea, and the invention of the tea bag.

Most people have heard about the Boston Tea Party. It happened on December 16, 1773, when American patriots disguised as Mohawk Indians threw 342 chests of tea belonging to the East India Company from their ships into the harbor in Boston. This protest concerned not only the tax on tea but also the perceived monopoly of the East India Company. The Boston Tea Party is one of the best-known historical moments associated with tea and one that would pave the way to the American Revolution and the Declaration of Independence in July 1776. Some would say that it also, in some ways, signaled the potential end to the tea-drinking habit that had been established up to that point; drinking or serving tea was seen to be unpatriotic. This event is largely why tea has never been part of the national identity of the United States of America.

Ironically it's partly because there have been no deep-rooted tea traditions that tea culture in the US today is thriving. Consumption of tea is on the rise: it's seen as a dynamic and exciting beverage with endless possibilities. The rich multiculturalism of the country means that the strong tea cultures of China, Japan, Eastern Europe, and Britain all influence how tea is now perceived. There are no limits to what can be done with tea: it's drunk hot or iced, pure and unadulterated, or with combinations of exotic flavors, as chai lattes, as "bubble" tea, and used in alcoholic cocktails and even more as an ingredient in cooking.

Numerous tea bars, ranging from the traditional kind influenced by European or Asian styles to more contemporary venues that compete with the most stylish and urban coffeehouses, are springing up across the nation, but particularly in the metropolitan cities on the East and West coasts. Green teas and herbal infusions are gaining in popularity as Americans look for potentially healthier alternatives to sodas and coffee. What is happening now in tea bars across the US is likely to influence the way tea is served worldwide.

 Who knew?

There is a place in New York state called Teatown. The name Teatown dates back to 1776 when tea was scarce, due to British taxation. A man named John Arthur moved to an area in northern Westchester after hoarding a chest full of tea, with ideas to sell it for a massive profit. A group of women called the Daughters of Eve discovered that he had a stash of tea and demanded a reasonable price; he refused, so the women besieged his home. After that, Mr. Arthur, in exchange for peace, agreed to sell the tea at a fair price. Now, the area is known as Teatown.

HOW TO MAKE: Iced tea

There are various ways of making iced tea. We certainly prefer the "fresh brewed" approach that uses real tea leaves rather than the sugary, instant tea powder sold in large tubs. In the southern states, a popular way to make iced tea is simply to place tea and cold water into a large glass jar or pitcher and let stand in the sun for 2 to 4 hours. Remove the tea and add ice and sugar if desired. See also page 195 for our favorite flavors of iced teas.

We prefer this much quicker way, which gives you freshly brewed iced tea in minutes.

1 Infuse some tea leaves in boiling water for 3 to 5 minutes in a glass or a pitcher; be sure to just cover the leaves with water to obtain a very concentrated infusion.

2 Then, remove the leaves and add iced water.

3 Garnish with fruit and a sprig of mint and it's ready to drink.

Unlike most countries in the world, over 80% of all the tea that is drunk in the US is drunk as iced tea. Some say that the origins of iced tea go back to 1904 during the World Fair in St. Louis, when Richard Blechynden, an enterprising English merchant, was in charge of the tea pavilion; however, due to the blistering heat of the day, he was having little success in attracting visitors. Somewhat desperate to show off his tea, he decided to serve it cold in glasses filled with ice. This proved to be an instant success and this is the moment that iced tea is said to have caught the attention of tea drinkers across the states. However, the true origins of iced tea appear to go back much further as tea-based drinks known as "punches" were common in southern states in the early 1800s. These "punches" were actually cocktails of green tea and alcohol. An early recipe for one such beverage appeared in an 1839 cookbook entitled *The Kentucky Housewife* where author Lettice Bryan suggested combining 1½ pints of strong tea, 2½ cups of white sugar, ½ pint of sweet cream, and a bottle of claret (dry red wine) or champagne. This beverage could be served hot or cold.

Other mentions of iced tea appeared in various other publications and as time moved on it seemed the most common way to drink tea would become black tea, with lemon and sugar over ice. In southern states, sweet iced tea is found everywhere, almost replacing water as the beverage of choice to help combat the intense summery heat. Tea doesn't come much more convenient than preprepared in a bottle, and ready-to-drink iced tea has become increasingly popular with sales now of over $5 billion. Now, that's an awful lot of iced tea.

While tea drinking is becoming even more popular, the US is certainly not renowned for growing tea; that said, tea is grown in South Carolina, Washington state, Alabama, and Hawaii. Probably the most significant tea plantations are in South Carolina, where the subtropical climate, ample rainfall, and sandy soils make great conditions for growing tea bushes. Tea was first successfully grown

Above Oh-so refreshing— freshly brewed iced tea.

in this region in the late 1880s but it wasn't until 1963 that a 127-acre (51.4-hectare) former potato farm on Wadmalaw Island was replanted with tea. Over the years, this has become a commercially viable tea estate, complete with factory and produces green and black teas.

Who knew?
In April 1995, South Carolina's grown tea was officially adopted as the Official Hospitality Beverage of the state.

Left Carnation milk, in first or last?

CANADA

While the vast majority of tea drunk in the US is iced, their northern neighbors in Canada have very different habits with the majority of tea consumption being hot. However, the vastness of Canada sees different tea preferences. On the West Coast most tea consumption is green tea and herbal; tea has very much been adopted as an alternative to coffee for many. Way out east in Newfoundland, tea is more traditional: the majority of tea is drunk as it is in Ireland (see page 26), strong and with milk. Carnation milk to be precise as Newfoundland lacks a major dairy industry. In between, pretty much anything goes with sophisticated tea bars enjoying success in cities such as Toronto and more French-style *salons de thé* experienced in Montreal.

INUIT TEA As well as strong black tea, the Inuit drink several herbal infusions. A tea known as Labrador tea (obviously from Labrador province not the dog!) is made from the leaves of a low-growing evergreen shrub. The leaves are used to make a tea rich in vitamin C that's best drunk as a weak brew as it has various toxic properties. Other herbal teas commonly associated with the frozen North include crowberry, juniper, and cloudberry, mostly drunk for medicinal reasons.

THE DANDELION
124 S 18th St, Philadelphia, PA 19103
www.thedandelionpub.com
When visiting Philadelphia's Rittenhouse Square neighborhood, The Dandelion is *the* destination for modern British gastropub cuisine. Their afternoon tea service, which is served everyday from 3 p.m. till 5 p.m., has something for every kind of tea fan! The "Queen's Croquet Ground" is a more traditional tea service that offers Twinings and teapigs. The "Mad Hatter Tea Party" menu caters to adventurous tea fans, of age of course, with unique tea cocktails such as Green Tea Mojito and Chamomile Lemonade with Bourbon. Lastly, "The Dormouse—High Tea for Tots" has caffeine-free teas and snacks such as peanut butter and grilled cheese sandwiches. The décor is whimsical and charming—try to get seated in the Dog Room!

MATCHABAR
93 Wythe Ave, Brooklyn, NY 11249,
www.matchabarnyc.com
Williamsburg, Brooklyn is a hub for hipsters and is always ahead of the curve, so it only makes sense that it's the home of NYC's first Matcha-only café—known, not surprisingly, as Matchabar. It serves traditional Matcha, as well as modern takes like lattes, "matchiatos" and iced peach Matcha. There is also an ever-changing food menu that includes crowd-pleasing items, such as Matcha donuts and muffins. Next time you are exploring Brooklyn, be sure to stop by for your Matcha fix!

SAMOVAR TEA BARS & LOUNGES
Four locations across San Francisco: The Mission, Hayes Valley, The Castro and Yerba Buena Gardens
www.samovartea.com
The team behind Samovar sees tea as a way to recharge and take a breather from the hustle and bustle of modern life. As soon as you walk in, the scent of spices from the chai tea being brewed in copper pots immediately grabs you and makes you forget about what's going on outside. It would be foolish to get your tea "to go" here. Instead, grab a seat and let the knowledgeable staff help you find exactly what you are

GRAB A TEA. USA & CANADA

looking for on their well-curated food and tea pairing menu. Samovar offers tea services from all over the world—Japan, England, Morocco, China, India, and Russia.

WOLFGANG PUCK AT HOTEL BEL-AIR
701 Stone Canyon Rd, Los Angeles, CA 90077
www.dorchestercollection.com/en/los-angeles/hotel-bel-air/restaurant-bars/wolfgang-puck-at-hotel-bel-air

If you looking for a way to spend a delightful afternoon in Los Angeles, then head out to the beautful and hidden oasis of Hotel Bel-Air for its afternoon tea service. The Hotel's slightly on the outskirts of town, toward Topanga State Park, so it may take a bit of time to get there, through the winding hills of Bel-Air, but it's totally worth it. You'll be instantly transported out of rush-hour traffic and into paradise. I recommend sitting outside to relax and take in that sunny Los Angeles weather. Afterward, explore the hotel's beautiful garden and pond—you may even see a swan or two waddling about!

THE BOULDER DUSHANBE TEAHOUSE
1770 13th Street, Boulder, CO 80302
www.boulderteahouse.com

The Boulder Dushanbe Teahouse in Boulder, Colorado, is one of the most special teahouses in the US. It was built as a gift from its sister city Dushanbe (in Tajikistan) with contributions from over 40 Tajikistani artists. With its vibrant, hand-carved ceilings in the interior and Boulder Creek running alongside the outdoor patio, the atmosphere here is a perfect blend of Tajikistan and local culture. It serves an afternoon tea every day 3 p.m. to 5 p.m. and sources tea from all corners of the world.

CEDERBERG TEA HOUSE
1417 Queen Anne Ave N, Seattle, WA 98109
www.cederbergteahouse.com

Although it's a city that is often synonymous with coffee, Seattle definitely has some amazing tea as well! One place to check out is Cederberg Tea House, especially if you are a rooibos fan! This South African café is known for its traditional-style rooibos lattes made with finely ground tea leaves in an espresso machine. And if you are hungry, there are great authentic bites, such as Bunny Chow and South African meat pies as well as a great selection of sweet treats.

TOWNSHEND'S TEA COMPANY
2223 NE Alberta St, Portland, OR 97211
www.townshendstea.com

What makes Portland such a special city is its sense of community and appreciation for craftsmanship. Townshend's Tea Company captures both! It features an incredibly well-curated tea menu with a cozy, welcoming ambience. With two locations in the city, it's a perfect place to get a sense of Portland's vibe. You can always find friendly locals inside and they feature local art and host shows for local artists and musicians. In the warmer months, they even put on outside catering (tea and food) for a mini-festival every month.

MANCAKES BAKERY
288 Robson St, Vancouver, BC V6B 6A1
www.mancakesbakery.com

Looking for a sweet treat with your cup? Pop in to ManCakes in Vancouver's hip Yaletown district. These guys sure know how to whip up a delicious cupcake. With at least 11 flavors daily like Bacon Chili Chocolate and Apple Brie, your taste buds are sure to be intrigued. Park yourself with your drink and cupcake of choice and surf the free Wifi or just spend some time people watching!

THE GREEN BEAN
210 Lakeshore Rd East, Oakville, ON L6J 1H8
www.greenbean.ca

Tucked away in scenic downtown Oakville, Ontario, The Green Bean offers a variety of coffees, teas, and treats. This little coffee- (or should we say tea-) house has a lovely patio for enjoying the beautiful summer, and sometimes spring and fall, weather. You can also bag a table inside or take your tea to go and explore historic Oakville and its lovely waterfront.

Below Samovar Tea Bar, the Mission branch.

ARGENTINA AND URUGUAY

Meet yerba mate (you say, "yerba-mat-hey"). Although not strictly a tea, like rooibos and other tisanes (see page 134), the leaves of the mate plant are often prepared in very much the same way as *Camellia sinensis*. Yerba mate is made from the leaves of a hollylike tree found in the rainforests of South America and particularly in northern Argentina, Uruguay, southern Brazil, and Paraguay. Mate was first consumed by the indigenous Guarani peoples and also spread to the Tupi people that lived in southern Brazil and Paraguay.

The leaves of the mate tree naturally contain vitamins, minerals, amino acids, and antioxidants. In fact, in the 1960s various scientific institutions concluded "it is difficult to find a plant in any area of the world equal to mate in nutritional value" and that yerba mate contains "practically all of the vitamins necessary to sustain life."

Yerba mate is drunk in many South American countries but none more so than in Uruguay and Argentina where it's pretty much the national drink. Many people carry a thermos of mate with them when they are out and about and there are hot water "refill" stations where the thirsty drinkers can top off.

Like many foodie traditions, the origins of mate are widely debated, but it's safe to assume that no trip to South America would be complete without experiencing one of the friendliest tea ceremonies around. Yerba mate is traditionally drunk out of a round bowl called a gourd and is often a shared experience as the gourd will be passed around among friends and family for everyone to sip from.

For centuries, rainforest tribes have drunk yerba mate for its ability to rejuvenate and provide focus. As a natural stimulant yerba mate is now becoming even more widely available, both in its traditional tea form but also in ready-to-drink formats.

While yerba mate is by far the most popular hot drink in Argentina, the country also enjoys traditional black tea and is a major tea producer, ranking ninth in the world in terms of production. Most tea in Argentina is grown in the northeastern provinces of Misiones and Corrientes where the climate is hot and humid and the land relatively flat, which allows for a highly mechanised form of harvesting and production. Argentina exports far more tea than it consumes domestically, with the vast majority going to the United States where it is most often used for iced tea.

Who knew?

To Argentinian gauchos (cowboys), yerba mate is known as "liquid vegetable"; while to native forest people it is known as the "drink of the Gods" as it has helped them survive periods of drought and famine.

HOW TO MAKE: A cup of yerba mate

1 Find a largish round cup (a real gourd if possible) and fill the cup two-thirds with the dried yerba mate leaves.

2 Cover the leaves with a little cold water—this protects the leaves.

3 Next, add hot water to fill the cup and let it steep.

4 Letting the leaves sit at the bottom of the cup, take a straw (a traditional gourd will have a *bombilla*, a strawlike filter) and pass it around.

5 Traditionally, the person preparing the mate known as the *cebador* will drink from the first infusion. They will then refill with hot water and pass counterclockwise between friends or family. When each person has had their fill they pass back to the *cebador* who refills the gourd and passes it to the next in the circle.

6 If you have had enough, say thank you and you won't be passed anymore (careful not to say thank you in advance of receiving or you might remain thirsty!).

Although it's often drunk as a social event, yerba mate can be consumed alone and, like Japanese Matcha (see page 112), it's common to see students with a thermos of water and a gourd by their side!

CHILE

Chile is the only country in South America that can be called a tea-drinking nation; it's also in the top 20 per capita tea-consuming countries (see page 18). This may stem from a peculiar teatime tradition inherited from the British, who settled in Chile in the 19th century. Teatime is firmly rooted in the food culture of Chile and there it's known as *onces*. It is said that this term dates back to the time when workers in mines run by the English would stop for tea in the afternoon, but here their tea break was accompanied by shots of *aguardiente*, a fierce "fire water" (not sure of the wisdom of drinking alcohol and working in a mine!). To disguise what they were drinking, the miners used the word *onces* and it caught on. In Chile today *onces* is as popular as it was a century ago. *Onces* is served anytime between 5 p.m. and 8 p.m.; it mostly consists of a plate full of lovely things to eat (sugary cakes, cookies, even pancakes with jam and fruit), of course all washed down with a lovely cup of black tea.

BRAZIL

Brazil is well known for its coffee culture, but if you're a tea lover, what would you do there? As a matter of fact, Brazil's tea culture comes from the indigenous cultures of the Amazon, with their infusions and medicinal herbs, and it has evolved since the Portuguese colonial period up to today. In the past five years there has been a spike in the arrival of specialist teashops, mostly in São Paulo. Now you can easily order green or white teas, or a tropical combination of tea with fruits and flowers to make it more refreshing and a bit unusual. We've spotted a few places to go and have a nice cup of tea, but be warned, Brazilians don't usually drink tea with milk. Just ask for some milk, if you like a drop of the white stuff, and enjoy it in a nice spot under the sun.

CAFÉ DEL PUENTE
Ernesto Riquelme 1180 B, Barrio Palafitos de Gamboa, Castro 5700315
www.mipalafitoapart.cl
This quaint Chilean teahouse, located in one of Castro's famous *palafitos* (wooden houses on stilts), offers gorgeous views over the water as well as an unrivaled selection of loose-leaf tea and cake! Described as a breakfast lover's dream, if you're in Chile then plan a trip here to enjoy the charming atmosphere and friendly welcome.

LAVANDA CASA DE TÉ
Quebrada Honda, Fundo Santa Marta, Frutillar
www.lavandacasadete.com
A true lavender heaven is the only way to really describe Chile's Lavanda Casa de Té and even then I'm not sure it really gives a true understanding of just how beautiful this place is! The teahouse itself is set among a vast lavender field, offering exquisite views as well as a tea menu of fine teas from all around the world. If you're after a relaxed atmosphere, unrivaled views and like taking tea in what is ultimately an adult's doll house, this could be for you! It is incredibly popular, so do book ahead.

AMARANTA TEA HOUSE
Avenida Cristóbal Colón 822 B, Punta Arenas 6200629
www.teamaranta.cl
This serene but cozy teahouse located in Punta Arenas, Chile, offers a number of artisan teas as well as a fab selection of cakes and pastries. Escape from a busy day and revel in some "me time" here. Enjoy some of their exciting blends of tea, including a fantastic chocolate tea, great for those looking to indulge without the guilt trip!

ALVEAR PALACE HOTEL
Avenida Alvear 1891, 1129AAA Buenos Aires
www.alvearpalace.com
In Argentina, Buenos Aires still holds the traditional 5 p.m. high tea in great esteem, and you can find it served in many of the city's finest hotels. The L'Orangerie restaurant within The Alvear Palace Hotel offers an extremely special afternoon tea, serving just the right kind of fabulous selection of tea and pastries. We recommend trying the hotel's own signature blend of tea, which aims to recreate the essence of the Alvear Palace Hotel!

TEALOSOPHY
Gorriti 4865, Buenos Aires
www.tealosophy.com
A tea-lover's dream—this unique little teashop rivals an old English candy store, but for tea! Each wall is covered from floor to ceiling with their vast range of teas; each in an individual tea caddy. The phenomenal aroma will hit you as soon as you walk through the door where the knowledgeable staff will be more than happy to help you choose your signature blend. A must for any tea fanatic!

TEA CONNECTION
Alameda Lorena 1271, São Paulo
www.teaconnection.com.br
This Argentinian teahouse chain has branched out in Brazil, Mexico, and Chile; it opened its first shop in São Paulo in 2010. Now, with two branches, you can choose from a nice range of tea blends and a great selection of fresh and healthy food that changes with every season. And the good thing is that if you're not sure how long to brew your tea, a chronometer will come with your teapot so you'll know exactly when your tea is ready. Genius!

THE GOURMET TEA
Rua Mateus Grou 89, São Paulo
www.thegourmettea.com.br
On arrival into this Brazilian shop you can tell it's something different; it has a unique concept, with its multicolored fold-out panels to reveal all kinds of tea treasures. With a great variety of teas displayed in cute and colorful tins, Gourmet Tea offers a menu with organic and fresh options, with bread and pasta made daily in their kitchen.

GRAB A TEA.
SOUTH AMERICA

AUSTRALIA

Pioneering tea growers, a cosmopolitan tea culture reflecting this continent's history and location, and a neat little invention that has become a Kiwi legend—that's what Australasia is in terms of the world of tea.

A form of tea from a plant called "ti tree" was drunk by Aboriginal Australians long before the country was "discovered" by foreigners, but tea as we know it (*Camellia sinensis*, see page 90) was introduced to Australia by the Brits. Tea was part of the cargo on what's known as the First Fleet, a flotilla of 11 ships that landed in Botany Bay in 1788 (having set off from Portsmouth, England, in May 1787) carrying a more famous "cargo," that of over 1,000 convicts.

Australia is also a small producer of tea and the history of tea growing there reflects the battling, pioneering spirit of the nation. In the late 1880s four young brothers, the Cutten brothers, planted tea, spices, coconuts, coffee, and numerous other tropical crops in an area that became known as Bingil Bay in tropical Northern Queensland. They suffered many trials and tribulations in attempting to establish a viable tea-growing business, but sadly in 1918 they were finally thwarted by a massive cyclone and tidal wave that hit the area destroying all of their crops.

That could have been the end of tea-growing downunder but in 1958 Dr. Allan Maruff, a migrant from India, planted tea seedlings in the area again and the first commercial tea-growing business in Australia was born. At the time, he discovered some of the remaining tea bushes from the earlier Cutten's attempts to cultivate, which by now had grown into trees some 49 feet (15m) high! Again, he faced many challenges, one of which was how to harvest the crop as there were no supplies of labor in the area to pluck the tea leaves. So, Dr. Maruff and a team of engineers developed mechanical harvesters to overcome this problem. He also built the first tea-processing factory in Australia, but sadly the venture was not a commercial success and the operation was closed down. Over the years, though, new investors were found and the business flourished. Today there are over 1,000 acres (405 hectares) of tea cultivation in the area, producing 3.3 million pounds (1.5 million kg) of black tea for consumption throughout Australia.

There is also some tea cultivation in New South Wales. In 1978, a third-generation tea planter from Sri Lanka called Michael Grant-Cook chose the Tweed Valley for its ideal climatic conditions and geographical resemblance to Assam, India. Tea here has flourished and in the late 1980s growers produced the first green tea in Australia. Green tea, specifically Japanese Sencha-style tea (see also page 110), is also produced in the upper reaches of the picturesque Kiewa Valley at Tawonga, Victoria.

The tea market in Australia reflects the modern cosmopolitan nature of its society. Traditional black tea with milk in the British style still predominates but green tea consumption is increasing, reflecting more of an Asian influence and, what's more, herbal infusions are also on the up, especially in the vibrant coffee bar scene that has developed in many cities, such as Melbourne.

Who knew?

Billy tea is the term used for making tea in a billy can (a lightweight cooking pot), made famous by the ill-fated swagman of *Waltzing Matilda* fame. "Billy up the fire" basically means "put the kettle on."

Left Billy tea on a boil.

Opposite Classic Thermette brewing.

NEW ZEALAND

Back in the late 1800s, New Zealand consumed more tea per capita than anywhere else in the world. The tea habit had started with tea being traded by the Chinese in return for seal skins. As the influence of the British Empire grew and tea cultivation developed in India and Sri Lanka, imports from those countries dominated. The tea culture developed very much along the same lines as in Britain, with tea gardens and the temperance movement both playing important roles.

This strong tea culture led to the invention of one of New Zealand's cultural icons—the Thermette. Invented in 1929 by John Hart, this device can boil enough water for 12 cups of tea in just 5 minutes using twigs or other combustible materials gathered from the great outdoors. "The stronger the wind, the better it boils," was one of Hart's early slogans, because wind sucks air up through the conical chimney inside the boiler from the base where the fire is lit. The sucking action makes the fire roar, and the heat is transferred not only to the base of the Thermette, but through the heated air rushing up the internal chimney. No heat is wasted; that is why the Thermette is so efficient. The Thermette became standard issue for the New Zealand army during the Second World War, where it became known as the "Benghazi boiler." While they aren't as widespread as they once were, the Thermette is still used by the New Zealand army and is still manufactured and sold to this day to tea drinkers who want the outdoor experience for brewing their tea.

THE HISTORY OF TEA

This page Lemongrass and ginger tea.

A tea timeline

As the second most drunk beverage in the world (after water), tea has obviously been around a while in order to establish its global fame. Its history involves revolutions, wars, political intrigue, the establishment of major trading routes, huge corporations, and plays no small part in the social history of many of the countries where it is popular. So, where did it all start?

LEGENDARY START

If tea is a legendary drink then its story must start with a legend, and it does. Way back in time, 2737BC to be precise, the leaves from a *Camellia sinensis* bush accidentally fell into a cauldron of boiling water belonging to Chinese emperor and herbalist Shen Nung. So impressed was he with the resulting brew that this new-found tea fast became a staple in Chinese culture.

   Over many centuries, cultivation of and trading in tea grew as did the importance of it in Chinese culture, as witnessed by the numerous ceremonies associated with its preparation and consumption. In the 8th century the first known book about tea was penned by a writer called Lu Yu; the book had a snappy little title, *Ch'a Ching*, roughly translated to *Classic of Tea*. It was around this time, too, that Japanese Buddhist monks studying in China took the beverage back to their homeland and thus initiated what was to become another huge ceremonial tea culture that continues to this day.

700 AD

2737 BC

Who knew?
Lu Yu's publication in 8th century China stated that there needs to be 24 implements used in the making of tea. No simple kettles or mugs would do in those days!

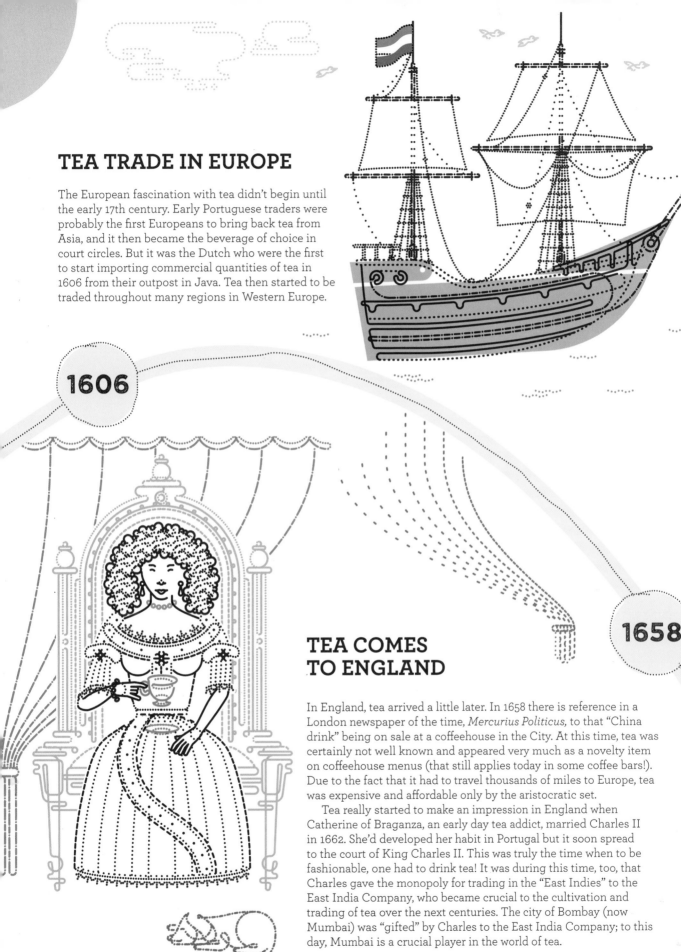

TEA TRADE IN EUROPE

The European fascination with tea didn't begin until the early 17th century. Early Portuguese traders were probably the first Europeans to bring back tea from Asia, and it then became the beverage of choice in court circles. But it was the Dutch who were the first to start importing commercial quantities of tea in 1606 from their outpost in Java. Tea then started to be traded throughout many regions in Western Europe.

1606

1658

TEA COMES TO ENGLAND

In England, tea arrived a little later. In 1658 there is reference in a London newspaper of the time, *Mercurius Politicus,* to that "China drink" being on sale at a coffeehouse in the City. At this time, tea was certainly not well known and appeared very much as a novelty item on coffeehouse menus (that still applies today in some coffee bars!). Due to the fact that it had to travel thousands of miles to Europe, tea was expensive and affordable only by the aristocratic set.

Tea really started to make an impression in England when Catherine of Braganza, an early day tea addict, married Charles II in 1662. She'd developed her habit in Portugal but it soon spread to the court of King Charles II. This was truly the time when to be fashionable, one had to drink tea! It was during this time, too, that Charles gave the monopoly for trading in the "East Indies" to the East India Company, who became crucial to the cultivation and trading of tea over the next centuries. The city of Bombay (now Mumbai) was "gifted" by Charles to the East India Company; to this day, Mumbai is a crucial player in the world of tea.

THE RUSSIAN CARAVANS

Most of the tea that came to Western Europe came by merchant ships, but for Russia the story was very different. Again, it was the late 17th century when tea started to be traded in Russia via the 11,000-mile trading route known as the Silk Road. The tea was transported in "caravans" that consisted of up to 300 camels, in a journey that could last up to 16 months. It is said that the Russian preference for "smoky" tea comes from the fact that the tea transported via this method was tainted by the smoke from the campfires; tea picks up nearby flavors. As in Western Europe, tea was very much the beverage for the wealthy few due to its high expense.

Who knew?

In the 1700s there was quite a debate about the suitability of tea for the working classes. A pamphlet published in 1758 entitled *The Good and Bad Effects of Tea Consider'd* made out that tea was fine for middle and upper classes but not so for "persons of an inferior rank and mean abilities." Snobbery at its worst; there was, of course, no meaningful reasoning to back this up. No airs, no graces, just fine tea for all, we say!

1689

TAXES, SMUGGLING, AND REVOLUTION

As with any product that is both expensive and popular, governments realized that there was money to be raised by taxing tea. Tea was first taxed in England in 1689. The high duties imposed and the growing popularity of tea led, of course, to a black market. The smuggling of tea became more and more prevalent to a point where more tea was smuggled in than was legally imported. One of the results of this was that the East India Company not only had reduced profits but also large stockpiles of tea. To help them, the British government granted exclusive trading rights in tea to the America colony, which also included the right to collect tax. To cut a long story short, this decision helped drive the revolutionary fervor in America where the local people rebelled against the imposition of taxes by "colonial masters." The Boston Tea Party on December 16, 1773, where tea from boats belonging to the East India Company was thrown into the harbor waters, is probably one of the best-known historical moments associated with tea. The stir that this event caused would ultimately lead to the American Revolution and Declaration of Independence in July 1776.

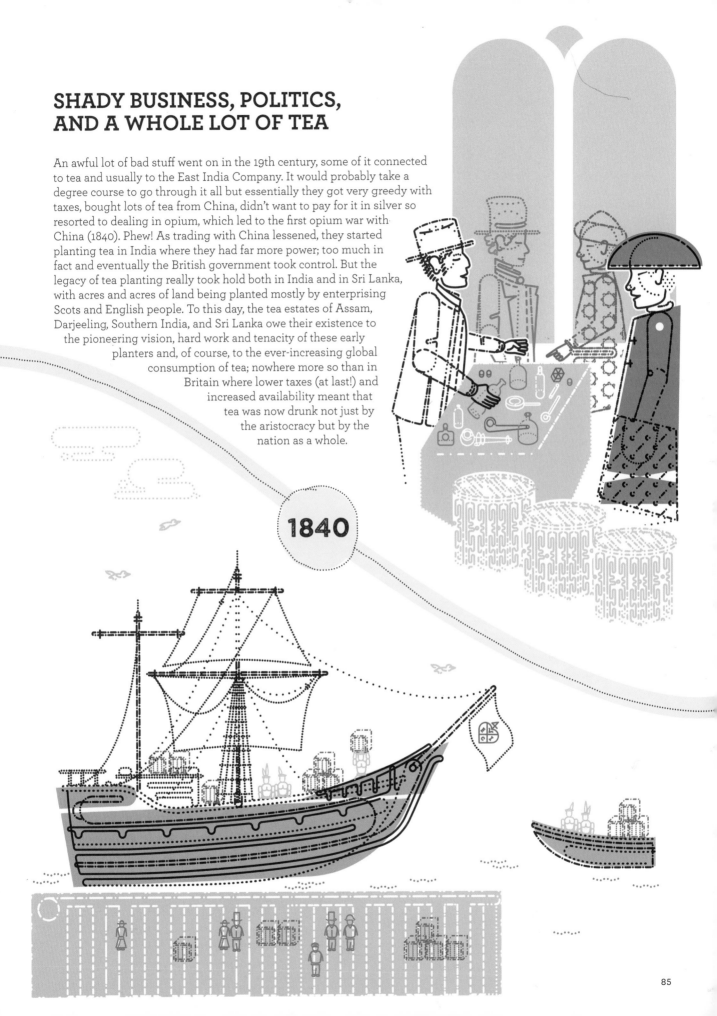

SHADY BUSINESS, POLITICS, AND A WHOLE LOT OF TEA

An awful lot of bad stuff went on in the 19th century, some of it connected to tea and usually to the East India Company. It would probably take a degree course to go through it all but essentially they got very greedy with taxes, bought lots of tea from China, didn't want to pay for it in silver so resorted to dealing in opium, which led to the first opium war with China (1840). Phew! As trading with China lessened, they started planting tea in India where they had far more power; too much in fact and eventually the British government took control. But the legacy of tea planting really took hold both in India and in Sri Lanka, with acres and acres of land being planted mostly by enterprising Scots and English people. To this day, the tea estates of Assam, Darjeeling, Southern India, and Sri Lanka owe their existence to the pioneering vision, hard work and tenacity of these early planters and, of course, to the ever-increasing global consumption of tea; nowhere more so than in Britain where lower taxes (at last!) and increased availability meant that tea was now drunk not just by the aristocracy but by the nation as a whole.

1840

THE RISE OF
THE TEA BAG

Global tea consumption continued to grow throughout the 20th century. Major companies, such as Lipton, Lyons, and Brooke Bond, developed tea brands and teashops in numerous countries. In the US the almost accidental invention of the tea bag (around 1908) led to tea becoming more popular due to it being easier and less messy to make. Thomas Sullivan, a New York tea merchant, sent samples of his tea to customers in small silken bags, which were mistakenly used by customers to actually brew the tea. Realizing he was onto something, Sullivan improved the bags, eventually using paper to contain the tea. It wasn't until the 1950s, after rationing from the Second World War had finished, that tea bags were introduced into Britain by Tetley. After a shaky start the British tea consumer became a fan of tea bags, they were after all so much more convenient. They are now used the world over, though loose tea does still play a big role in many tea cultures. Today, the tea bag continues to be popular, but some manufacturers are experimenting with other shapes of tea bag and other materials to contain the tea, other than paper.

1908

TEA IN THE 21ST CENTURY

So, some 4700-odd years after those leaves fell into the pot of Emperor Shen Nung, and despite the challenges of coffee, beer, wine, and soft drinks to name but a few, tea continues to play a major role in the world and in modern-day society. The use of herbal teas or tisanes, also steeped in centuries of tradition and folklore, along with the ever-popular brews from the tea plant *Camellia sinensis* mean that more and more people are enjoying the delights of tea, whether it is hot, iced, in a naughty cocktail or two, or maybe even as an ingredient in cooking. There is also an increasing trend toward tea bars in cities worldwide where tea lovers can enjoy their favorite brew while connecting with people all around the globe.

Who knew?
George Orwell, better known for his political novels also wrote a very important piece about how to make the perfect cup of tea, involving 11 golden rules. Not sure we'd be too relaxed making him a brew!

TEA HISTORY AT A GLANCE

2737 BC
Tea discovered by Emperor Shen Nung in China.

8TH CENTURY
Chinese writer Lu Yu writes *Ch'a Ching*, the first-ever book on tea.

1607
First major import of tea from Asia to Europe by the Dutch.

1658
The first mention of tea published in a paper referring to the "China drink" in a coffee bar in the City of London.

1662
Tea addict Catherine of Braganza marries Charles II and tea starts to become popular (within court circles only) in England.

1680-90s
The Silk Road caravans establish a tea trade with Russia.

1689
The first tea tax is levied in England.

1773
The mother of all tea parties happens in Boston.

1784
Tax on tea is dramatically reduced by the British government, from 119% to 12%; unsurprisingly, legitimate tea sales grew.

1839-1842
The first opium war rages between China and Britain—a result of dubious business practices.

1850s
Tea planting expands into India and Sri Lanka.

1888
British tea imports from India exceed those from China for the first time.

1908
The invention of the tea bag by Thomas Sullivan.

1980s
Invention of the pyramidal mesh bag by NASA/Fuso industries in Japan for whole-leaf green tea.

2015
Tea remains the number one hot drink in the world.

FROM PLANT TO POT

This page White tea.

What exactly is tea?

All tea comes from the leaves of the *Camellia sinensis* plant; you'll see later that when we talk of rooibos or herbal teas these are really tisanes or infusions. So, if it's called tea, it must come from the *Camellia sinensis* plant: a subtropical evergreen plant—related to the camellia, which can be found in gardens. There are two main varieties that are recognized: *Camellia sinensis* var. *sinensis* traditionally found in China and *C. sinensis* var. *assamica* traditionally found in Assam, India (the clue is in the species name).

But the type of camellia is just the start of it. Like wine, tea is divided into regional and individual estate varietals (up to 1,500) and manufacturing styles, all of which contribute to the huge variety of tastes and colors of different teas. For example, you will only find the very best Darjeeling black tea growing in the foothills of the Himalayas. Alternatively, the traditional fermentation and drying methods uniquely used in Taiwan produces the special flavor of Tung Ting oolong (see also page 116).

All tea starts off as buds or leaves on a tea bush but with the way it's plucked and processed you can end up with a staggering array of different teas, from white tea to dark pu-erh tea. We think it is amazing that one plant can produce so many unique flavors and tastes. The taste variation starts in the growing of the plant—the location, the soil, the altitude, and the weather patterns (see also pages 92 and 94). The way the leaves are treated after plucking changes the final flavor of the tea; there is a whole vocabulary dedicated to describing tea flavors— see our attempt to simplify tea-geek speak (see pages 122–123).

A good tea is a well-made tea—one that has been looked after and finely crafted. Very generally tea estates have to choose between making large volumes of "alright" tea or a smaller amount of something really top-notch. If they choose the latter they will only pluck the best leaves (the freshest shoots from the top of the bush) and process them very delicately ensuring that they don't damage the leaf. (More on this later, see The journey of a tea leaf, pages 98–103.)

Opposite Tea pluckers in Darjeeling, India.

Camellia sinensis var. sinensis

LIKES Cold and steep mountains (up to 8,530 feet/2,600m)
MAKES Tiny, delicate leaves for mostly green, white, and Darjeeling teas
NATIVE TO China
HEIGHT 5 to 15 feet (1.5 to 4.5m) if left to its own devices
LEAF SIZE 2 inches (5cm)
SEASON Because it is clinging to a mountainside, the growing season is spring/summer
PLUCKING About five times a year

Camellia sinensis var. assamica

LIKES Rain, warmth, and space to grow
MAKES Black tea; big, tough leaves more similar to the garden camellia; used in all the big tea-growing regions (India, China)
NATIVE TO Assam, India
HEIGHT Up to 60 feet (18m)!
LEAF SIZE 8 inches (20cm)
SEASON All year
PLUCKING Every 8 to 12 days!

Above Green leaf tea being weighed.

How is tea grown?

As tea has been grown and harvested for hundreds of years, the arrangement of tea bushes and their plucking—that's the correct term for the picking of the leaves—is now down to quite a fine art. For instance, every tea bush is grown from a cutting or clone, which is carefully nurtured in nursery beds until it and all of the other clones are ready for planting out; a process that can take six to eight months. Young bushes are planted about 5 feet (1.5m) apart in rows with a distance of 3⅓ feet (1m) between each row. In the higher altitudes, these rows follow the contours of the hills or mountainsides or are grown along terraces to avoid eroding the soil. Tea bushes are allowed to grow until they're about 3⅓ feet (1m) high and then they're kept at that height, which makes for easier plucking.

The tea bush itself is trained into a fan shape, with a flat top called a plucking table. This handy area for plucking the best leaves spans an area of about 3⅓ x 5 feet (1 x 1.5m) and it takes between three and five years of plucking and shaping to come to full maturity, meaning that tea can then be produced from the leaves. The *Camellia sinensis* var. *assamica* is harder to train; you are fighting its natural desire to become a 60-foot (18-m) tree—but when it reaches 20 inches (50cm), its center stem is cut to push the growth outward rather than upward.

Once the tea bush is up and running and has its plucking table established, the bushes are plucked at regular intervals. When we say plucked, what we mean is that the top two leaves and a bud are plucked from the sprigs of the plucking table. The regularity of this plucking depends on the variety, location, altitude, and weather. Generally, the *Camellia sinensis* var. *assamica* is plucked very regularly, mostly by hand, every 7 to 14 days; however, in peak season when there is a lot of rain, the bushes could be ready for plucking again within just 2 to 3 days. On the other hand, the *Camellia sinensis* var. *sinensis* is slower growing, partly as a result of the locations it's grown in, is more delicate, and therefore much less demanding; it only requires plucking four or five times per growing season.

Tea-plucking seasons vary by the particular varietal of tea grown, the weather, and geographical location (see also pages 94 and 96). Some of the tea-growing regions are very seasonal—winter (cold), summer (hot)—while those hugging the Equator tend to have seasons defined by the arrival of rains, which generate flushes of growth.

THE HIGH-TECH APPROACH TO GROWING TEA

Japanese tea production is slightly unusual because of the sophisticated high-tech approach that many Japanese tea planters have. Large areas, particularly around the Kagoshima Prefecture, are harvested by machines rather than people. The tea bushes are pruned to form a fanlike shape rather than the more usual table. These rounded sides work well with the machines. The tea bushes are planted 67in (170cm) apart to allow the machines to move in between. The result of this unusual planting is the most beautifully neat rows of tea (see page 111). Frost is a challenge the world over, but the Japanese use shade, sprinklers, and fans (to blow cold air away) to protect their tea bushes—some people may think that this ruins the look of the tea fields but, in fact, it protects the planters' crops from damage. And we're all for top-notch crops.

PERFECT GROWING CONDITIONS FOR TEA

VERY WET SUMMERS
about 39in (100cm) annual rainfall it takes 32 pints/18.4 liters) to produce enough leaves to brew a cup of tea)

SUNSHINE AND DRY WINTERS

EVEN TEMPERATURES YEAR ROUND

LIGHT SHADE

DEEP, SLIGHTLY ACIDIC SOIL

Where is tea grown?

In its wild state, tea grows best in regions that enjoy a warm, humid climate with a rainfall measuring at least 39 inches (100cm) a year—typically, that's the region between the Tropic of Cancer and the Tropic of Capricorn. Ideally, tea bushes like deep, light, acidic, and well-drained soil. Given these conditions, tea will grow in areas from sea level up to altitudes as high as (and even above) 8,500 feet (2,600m) above sea level. You can find tea growing just off the coast road in Sri Lanka, as well as at Kolukkumalai near Munnar in India, which claims to be the highest tea plantation at 8,150 feet (2,484m) above sea level.

Above Plucker in Assam, India, taking a rest, shelters from the rain under her umbrella..

The big players in the world of tea growing are China, India, Sri Lanka, and Kenya, followed by Turkey, Vietnam, Iran, and Indonesia, but this is by no means an exhaustive list: tea can be grown in any area with the right climate and conditions.

As a tea taster a fun list of "work trips" could be drawn up from the lesser-known tea-producing regions—starting with Hawaii. While tea is grown in other areas of the US (Mississippi, Washington, South Carolina), Hawaii has a number of successful tea estates, including the Rainforest Tea estate where tea plants/bushes grow in the shade of the rainforest and on lava rock base (see also page 107). Mauritius, one of the smallest tea-producing regions, has grown tea since 1892. Cornwall in the UK is one of the newest tea-growing areas; its microclimate has made growing tea possible since 2000. High up in the Andes of Ecuador, at nearly 3,000 feet (914m) above sea level, tea has been grown since the 1960s; they produce black tea year round at the Sangay tea estate. China is the largest producer of tea—in 2013, it produced 2,039,276 tons; meanwhile India came in second with 1,322,818 tons.

> There are those who love to get dirty and fix things. They drink coffee at dawn, beer after work. And those who stay clean, just appreciate things. At breakfast they have milk and juice at night. There are those who do both, they drink tea.
>
> Gary Snyder, *American poet*

Who knew?
For the consumption of China's annual 550 billion cups of tea, China uses 236,588 Olympic-size swimming pools worth of water.

Who grows tea?

You may have heard of coffee plantations but when it comes to growing tea much of the world's tea is grown on what are known as tea estates and smallholdings. The difference between the two is mainly one of size.

Above A tea farmer drying tea leaves in Pein Ne Bin village, Shan region, Myanmar.

A smallholding, sometimes referred to as a tea garden (see page 124), for example, is privately owned and can be as small as 1.2 acres (0.5 hectare) or can cover several hectares. To give you an idea of size, 1 acre is 4,840 square yards (or the size of a soccer pitch). Where tea is grown on smallholdings, there are tea cooperatives that build a tea-processing factory central to a group of smallholders. The owners of the smallholdings sell their plucked leaves (called green leaf) to the factory for processing.

A tea estate, on the other hand, is a self-contained unit, often hundreds of hectares in size, housing its own factory, tea-growing area, schools, hospital, staff houses and gardens, places of worship, reservoir, and guest houses; see for example the Happy Valley Estate, page 126.

Frequently a tea estate will also accept green leaf from smallholders. So, someone living in a tea-growing region with spare land can begin production and then sell their green leaf to the local tea estate; this is a pretty common practice. The role that

a tea estate has in rural communities cannot be underestimated. Tea-growing regions are often remote and lacking in any type of infrastructure. The growing of tea is central to the development of these areas, providing a livelihood and incorporating healthcare and education.

There are large estate groups in the big tea-producing countries, who manage a number of estates. Mcleod Russell is the largest, owning tea estates in India, Vietnam, Rwanda, and Uganda —this estate group produces over 1.1 million tons of tea each year.

TOP 20 TEA PRODUCERS

1700

CHINA

1000

INDIA

369.4

KENYA

330

SRI LANKA

Who produces more tea than any other nation? It's China, of course—where tea was first discovered way back in history. This gives the expression "for all the tea in China" some real meaning. We salute you China for producing so much of our favorite drink. (Figures in metric tonnes; source UN 2013.)

TURKEY 2.25	**VIETNAM** 216.9	**IRAN** 158
INDONESIA 150.1	**ARGENTINA** 100	**JAPAN** 85.9
		THAILAND 75
BANGLADESH 61.5	**MALAWI** 53.5	**UGANDA** 50.9
		TANZANIA 32.8
MYANMAR 32	**RWANDA** 22.5	**MOZAMBIQUE** 22
ZIMBABWE 19	**NEPAL** 18.7	

THE JOURNEY OF A TEA LEAF

One of the most amazing tea facts is that all tea comes from the same plant. The transformation from green leaf to "made tea" (tea that you can actually drink) is all down to the tea experts who process the leaves in tea factories, large and small, around the world. Below, we take you on the journey from small, bright-green leaf to tea in your favorite mug.

Plucking

Tea plucking is the most crucial stage (see also page 92) as the rule is you can't make good tea from a badly plucked tea leaf. The majority of tea is still plucked by hand the tea-plucking machines used are not as accurate as nimble fingers. The plucker on a good tea estate is aiming to pick the top two leaves and a bud from the tea bush: these are the fresh shoots. To make sure that the finest leaves are always picked, the pluckers move around the rows of tea bushes in a plucking round a bit like mowing a lawn, starting on one side and finishing on the other.

The plucked leaves are collected in a basket or bag carried on the back of the plucker, and when this is full it is taken to a collection point where the plucked leaf is weighed and the standard of the leaf is checked. The different quality of leaf is separated (two leaves and a bud/three leaves and a bud, and so on) to make sure the correct standard goes to the factory for processing, or "making" as tea manufacture is known in the tea trade.

A skilled plucker can gather between 66 and 77 pounds (30 and 35kg) of plucked leaf in a day – that's enough to produce about 13 to 15 pounds (6 to 7kg) of processed black tea.

Processing the tea once it's plucked is a skillful and time-consuming job. Over the next few pages, we look at all the various "treatments" a tea leaf could be subject to on its journey from tea bush to teapot.

Withering

The leaves are in the tea factory within 12 hours of plucking and the withering process begins. This is basically when the moisture content of the leaf is reduced —a slightly shriveled leaf is the result. The leaves are laid over open mesh; in larger factories ambient air is blown under the leaves. The leaves physically wilt and the moisture content of the leaf drops to below 70%. The factory manager won't test this, he will just know! His experience will tell him that when he squeezes the wilted green leaf in his hand whether the moisture content is reduced enough. The physical wither shows that the leaf is now soft, pliable, and ready for rolling; the chemical wither, which has occurred inside the leaf itself, means that the aromatics and volatile compounds inside the leaf have been released, which will produce the flavor. The withered leaves are now ready for the next stage of processing.

Rolling

The next stage is all about getting the juicy flavors open to the elements (breaking the leaf). There are two ways to do this: what's known as the orthodox method or the cut tear curl method, or CTC for short.

Orthodox method

This traditional method replicates rolling a green leaf gently between your palms. The leaf is fed onto a rolling table from above, a ridge plate above moves off the table, gently twisting the leaf. The buds retain their shape and do not break—these are the finest tips.

The twisted leaf is then fed over a sorter and the different grades of leaf are sorted; the finest leaf is removed and the second or third sort remain on the orthodox table. The quality decreases the longer the leaf is on the table.

Cut tear curl (CTC)

This process is best for tea destined for tea bags, as the smaller surface area means a faster brew. The soft leaf is first passed through a pair of rollers that have tiny teeth, which cut the leaf and roll it into small pieces.

Both orthodox and CTC methods break the leaf and release the enzymes from inside the tea leaves. The enzymes (contained within the remaining moisture of the leaf, a kind of juice really) hold all the flavor and aroma, which will make the tea taste great.

Oxidation

In the world of tea we call this fermentation. Essentially the oxidation process is the leaf turning brown. Much like leaving a freshly cut apple open to the elements, it turns from fresh pale green to brown. In terms of technical details, it's at this stage that the theaflavin and thearubigin chemicals are created. These substances give the tea briskness and strength. It is a delicate balance to get this stage correct; underfermented tea tastes light and green, while overfermented tea can taste stewed.

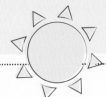

Steaming, pan–firing, or drying

The aim of this last part of the process is to get the moisture content below 3%. This dehydration stops the oxidation process in its tracks and so stabilizes the taste of the tea. Whether it's done in a steamer, pan, or under the sun depends on the type of tea you want to produce.

↓

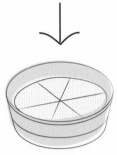

Sorting or grading

The bulk tea is sorted by passing through sorters and is graded as: whole leaf, broken, and fannings. For more on this process, see pages 122–123.

↓

Packing

Most of the tea estates still transport the tea in bulk, rather than packing into a consumer-ready product on the tea estate itself. To retain their freshness, the teas are packed into Kraft paper, foil-lined sacks—no more tea chests, I'm afraid. The sacks of tea are then stacked on pallets and then they're ready for sale.

Different tea, different steps

Not all tea is the same. All tea does come from green leaf but what you get at the end depends on the processes the leaf goes through. Here's a handy summary.

WHITE TEA

White tea is basically unprocessed tea and is named after the fuzzy white "down" that appears on the buds. White tea is simply plucked and then left to dry. A bit of oxidation does happen naturally, as it can take 24 hours to air-dry the tea leaves, which explains why some white teas have different colored leaves—from white to green. White teas should have a very pale green or yellow liquor—they are superlight teas.

GREEN TEA

Green tea is plucked, withered, and rolled. Heat is applied to stop any oxidation happening —this heat is what makes the tea green. The green leaf is either steamed or pan-fired (tossed in a hot wok) to a temperature hot enough to stop the enzymes from browning the leaf. At the same time as this heating, the leaves are twisted or flattened in the wok. To finish the process the leaf is dried. Green tea is green and its taste profile varies hugely—pan-fried teas taste more toasty while the steamed teas are more vegetable in taste.

OOLONG TEA

Oolong tea is semioxidized and generally sits between black and green tea. It covers all elements of the basic tea production and then some. The rolling and oxidizing stages are repeated. The amount of oxidation ranges from 10% to 80%—this can only be broadly assessed by the amount of brown color in the leaf. The time and complexity involved in making oolong teas is shown in the wow wow wow! flavor that oolong teas have—fruity and flowery.

BLACK TEA

Black tea covers all the steps too, from plucking all the way through to sorting and packing. The most important stage for this type of tea is the fermentation, when the leaf oxidizes. Finally, the leaf is cooked in a giant oven to seal in the flavor.

Who knew?

Some tea bag-making machines can produce about 2,000 paper tea bags in just 1 minute. So, if the machine ran nonstop all day, that's not far off 3 million tea bags!

The tea can then take a couple of different routes to the end consumer.

Auction houses

The traditional route for tea is for it to be sold via an auction house. Tea auction houses are in Kenya, Malawi, India (North and South), and Indonesia. Ahead of the weekly auctions, a sample of the batch of tea is dispatched to the various buyers for tasting in advance. The buyers then come together, having earmarked their lots, and then bid on the teas lot by lot. The fact that the same buyers are present on a weekly basis results in a wonderfully lively atmosphere!

Private sales

Some teas are purchased directly between the tea estate and the end consumer. In such sales, predominantly tea brokers are still used; these brokers act as the knowledgeable "middle men" who understand the quality of the tea and the market. These private sales can be linked to the auction prices or in certain scenarios (most notably, for premium teas) are driven by supply and demand.

Once purchased the tea is then shipped to its final destination, where it will be packed into a consumer-ready format. The majority of teas are shipped rather than air freighted.

In the UK, 96% of tea is consumed in a tea bag format, so the majority of tea headed to British shores is destined for a tea bag-packing machine before it makes it to the consumer.

Tea bags are now produced in a range of shapes to maximize flavor, but loose, whole-leaf tea is clearly the best. Innovations on the tea bag front are a biodegradable mesh to contain the leaves, as well as a three-dimensional shape to allow better brewing. See also page 151.

Types of tea

If you want to become more of a knowledgeable tea American or just want to discover some wonderful old stories about tea, then read on. Here, we take you on a whistle-stop tour of all five types of true tea—white, oolong, green, black, and pu-erh—followed up by the herbal teas (rooibos, chamomile, peppermint, yerba mate, and the like).

WHITE TEA

Tea or not tea? It's tea as it comes from the *Camellia sinensis* plant
Where is it grown? Fuding, China
How does it taste? Delicate and subtle
How to make? Brew for 3 minutes
How to serve? Hot without milk
What makes it special? It's hardly processed at all

White tea has almost nothing done to it (see what little happens to it in The journey of a tea leaf, pages 98–101 and 102). Genuine white tea originates from the Fujian province, in the area around a Chinese city called Fuding. While the city itself is not that exciting (although I had the most amazing fish soup there on one of my visits), the hills and mountains surrounding the city are stunning, and in parts the soft green tea bushes are interspersed with sharp rock faces.

While other regions around the world (for example, Sri Lanka, Darjeeling, Southern India, Kenya, and Hawaii) have copied the process of white tea production, it is commonly felt that "genuine" white tea has to come from Fujian province. It has to be said, though, that there are some great and interesting flavors coming from these other regions, too.

The tea bushes grown in this region are a particular cultivar of *Camellia sinensis* called Dai Bai—also known as the great white cultivar. The bushes lie dormant through the winter months until spring arrives between mid-March and mid-April. The tips of the tea bush are picked as soon as the first sign of spring appears. The shoots are coated in tiny, downy hairs—in the past, we have had a few customers complain of "fluff" on their tea, but this is what gives white tea its name and is actually a sign of great white tea!

The first two weeks of production are the most precious, valuable, and delicate. The leaves are not cut or allowed to oxidize, they are traditionally dried in the sun but can be dried on racks inside during poor weather. Rain is the biggest danger to the tea as it can damage the delicate leaf at the time of plucking, ideally the leaves are plucked early in the morning in warm sunshine.

The most popular white teas are Silver Needle and White Peony.

SILVER NEEDLE TEA
The top-grade white tea—Bai Hao Yin Zhen—is known as "silver needle" or "silver tips" and is the most expensive tea. This tea looks like silver needles (you'd never guess from the name, would you?!) and are just the shoots or single tips of the tea bush and no lower leaf whatsoever. This tea gives the lightest flavor and clearest liquor of any tea. It tastes slightly sweet, some say like honeysuckle.

WHITE PEONY TEA
Second in line is Bai Mu Dan (sometimes spelled Pai Mu Tan) and translates as "white peony"; it gets its name from the way that the tea leaves appear to bloom like spring flowers when the tea is brewed.

This grade of tea has two leaves and a bud. It still contains the silver needle but is accompanied by its two lower leaves. These lower leaves give the tea a stronger and more complex flavor. Again, the leaves are processed in a very delicate way to minimize breakage, which prevents oxidation and helps the leaf to retain its super-light character. Bai Mu Dan's flavor has slightly more melon to it. Some people prefer Bai Mu Dan to the Bai Hao Yin Zhen because it does deliver a stronger taste.

 Who knew?
An old Chinese tale about white tea tells that the tea bushes were plucked for two weeks each year in the spring (true) by young virgins and the tea buds were rolled and dried in the sun (partly true).

Opposite Chinese tea plucker in Fujian province, picking early season white tea.

meet the tea maker

Louise meets … Jenny Ruan a white tea farmer from Fuding, China. Her family has been working in the tea business for more than 20 years. Their tea factory was founded in 1992 and is involved in tea planting, processing, and research.

Where in the world?
Fuding, Fujian province, China

At what altitude does it sit?
About 1970 to 3940 feet (600 to 1200m) above sea level

How much tea does it produce? About 28 tons per year

How many workers?
About 60 full-time employees and 400 seasonal workers

What types of tea are produced?
White tea, green tea, black tea, jasmine tea, and oolong tea

Describe your estate?
We grow tea up on the hills around Fuding but it's about an hour's drive to our nearest town, so we are fairly remote.

How have you seen the tea industry change? How have the requirements changed for tea growers?
The tea industry has changed a lot in the past 20 years. Before that, nearly all the tea companies and tea factories were state-owned. Nowadays most of them are private. We see the Chinese market growing rapidly year on year. It seems that tea drinking is becoming ever more popular; and people are willing to pay much more for top-quality teas. It used to be that white tea was mainly exported, but in recent years, the domestic demand for white tea has been high. People believe that drinking white tea is much better for their health than other kinds of tea. On the other hand, it becomes more and more difficult to find workers to do the hard work, such as plucking tea, sorting etc., as the youngsters are all off to the cities.

Can you describe a typical day on the estate?
It's pretty nonstop. There's checking the quality of fresh tea leaves, checking tea processing, and tasting the tea, to name but a few jobs. During the production season, we stay mostly on the tea estate to focus on the production. When the production season finishes, we have more freedom. Our tea bushes are plucked from the middle to the end of March—the last two weeks only. People pluck the fresh tea leaves very tenderly by hand and then extract buds one by one. There are somewhere between 25,000 and 28,000 tea buds in 2¼ pounds (1kg) of silver needle tea.

What do you love about tea?
I think that tea is the most healthy drink in the world. The environment of the tea bushes is free from pollution and the soil is perfect for supporting the tea growth. I like to refresh myself with a cup of good tea. Usually we just drink our own tea, but sometimes we exchange and share some good teas with other friends in the tea business.

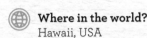

meet the tea maker

Louise meets … Bob Jacobson, President of Hawaii Rainforest Tea and President of the Hawaii Tea Society. Bob has been into tea growing only since 2008 but in that time has instigated the growing of tea in the rainforests of Hawaii along with setting up a nonprofit organization for small tea growers in the surrounding islands.

Where in the world?
Hawaii, USA

At what altitude does it sit?
About 1,000 feet (300m) above sea level

How much tea does it produce? In 2014, we produced 33 pounds (15kg) of white tea

How many workers?
At the moment, just me; plus I get occasional workers to help me weed

What types of tea are produced?
Organic white tea

Describe your estate?
My farm lies about 15 miles from Hilo, the biggest town on our island, in the middle of a tropical rainforest. To get to the farm, you have to drive along gravel roads through remote areas—there are a few houses dotted around and about—but we're nestled in among fantastic native rainforest, which is growing on lava that flowed 300 to 600 years ago. We harvest our water from the rain and we power the farm with solar electricity.

What got you into tea?
I founded my farm with my first plantings in 2008. But my journey into the world of tea began as I traveled to tea-growing areas of the world, such as Kenya and China. I had an idea that you could grow tea as an understory crop beneath the rainforest canopy and that such a scale of growing could be undertaken by small family farms; in turn, this would help preserve our natural rainforests.

What is great about the tea grown in Hawaii and why?
Hawaii tea does not become bitter when brewed for a long time; the flavor we produce is unique to Hawaii. It took about two years to find exactly the right handling to give my white tea its superb flavor. The strength of the tea seems to increase each year.

How have you seen the tea industry change? How have the requirements changed for tea growers?
Before now there wasn't much of a tea industry in Hawaii. My tea is a niche product because it is grown in Hawaii, it is certified organic, it is hand plucked, and estate processed. It doesn't compare easily to any other tea.

What manufacturing processes do you use at your estate?
I only produce a white tea. It is plucked and immediately heat treated in a 104°F (40°C) oven.

Can you describe a typical day on the estate?
My tea grows on the ground beneath the native ohia and kopiko trees of the rainforest. I weed, pull off flowers, buds, and seeds from the 6,000 to 7,000 plants that grow on the farm—about 1.5 acres (0.6 hectare). But even the process of weeding delights me: I work with accompanying birdsong and get surprising and brief glimpses of orchids and other rainforest gems that I discover; every day is different.

How often do you leave the tea estate?
I stay on my farm most of the time. I visit other islands in Hawaii to visit family and do business about once a month. In the past I have visited tea-growing areas in China, Taiwan, and Kenya, but these days I travel out of Hawaii about once a year for family and business obligations.

What's your favorite cup? Do you only drink your own tea?
My favorite beverage is my own white tea. However, I like most teas if they are of good quality.

How do you drink tea? Do you only drink freshly brewed tea?
I drink all quality teas that are available, freshly brewed. I love tea.

What do you love about tea?
Tea gives me the clarity of mind described in the earliest literature on tea. White tea tastes wonderful.

GREEN TEA

Tea or not tea? It's tea as it comes from the *Camellia sinensis* plant
Where is it grown? China and Japan
How does it taste? From light and floral (good) to astringent vegetable (not so good)
How to make? Brew for 3 minutes
How to serve? Hot without milk
What makes it special? Its amazing diversity

Part of what makes green tea special is its complexity. While green tea is now grown all over the world, China and Japan remain the top producers.

About 75% of green tea is still produced in China, and different regions and individual producers grow very different types of green tea. The country is dominated by small producers, each producing their own take on tea, traditionally produced by hand (and that is still common today). There are styles of tea associated with each region, however each producer has tweaked and perfected their production to give a different result. There are also some lovely stories (true or not, we don't know but we love them all the same) that have built up over the years that make the Chinese green teas even more magical. Read on to find out more.

The basic process of heating the withered tea leaves to stop the oxidation from happening (see page 100) is what makes a green tea. How this is done defines the green tea. Green tea is either steamed or pan-fried to halt oxidation and keep the fresh-green look of the leaves. Heating removes moisture and readies the leaf for rolling, twisting, and drying.

There are some big hitters in the world of green tea. First, the Chinese green teas, then the Japanese ones.

CHINESE GREEN TEAS

There are lots of green teas from China, but here we let you in on the secret of our favorite four.

DRAGON'S WELL LONG JING
Originating from near Hangzhou, the capital of Zhejiang province in China, this tea is pan-fried. It's full name is Long Jing, which translates as Dragon's well. The leaf has a distinctive flat needle shape and the taste is sweet and slightly toasty.

MAO FENG
Mostly grown in Anhui and Zhejiang provinces, Mao Feng has a light and peachy taste. To give it its full name, this tea is Huang Shan Mao Feng, which translates as "downy point of the yellow mountain."

GUNPOWDER
This is a classic green tea from China's Zhejiang province. Gunpowder tea is rolled by hand into small balls or pellets—making them look like old-fashioned balls of gunpowder. The smoky character of gunpowder is very distinctive; you'll find it's also drunk in Morocco but there is partnered by lots of mint and considerable quantities of sugar.

CHUNMEE
Also known as "precious eyebrows," Chunmee is a Chinese green tea with a distinctive eyebrow-shaped leaf, originating from Jiangxi province. This tea is less smoky than a traditional gunpowder but tends not to have the complex, delicate flavors of some of the more premium green teas.

> **YELLOW TEA** This unique Chinese tea starts as a green tea but after the pan-firing the leaves are heaped under cloth. The resultant heat and humidity turns the leaves yellow and gives the brew a mellow, sweet taste.

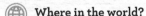

meet the tea maker

Louise meets ... Shi Hong Fang, Tea Manager at the Yi Xing Ming Ling Xiang Zhen Tea Garden near Li Xing in Eastern China. Unlike some really remote tea gardens or estates, this tea garden is walkable from the nearest village, being about 1¼ miles (2km) away.

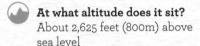

Where in the world?
Zhang Zhu Yi Xing province, China (about a 2½-hour drive West from Shanghai)

At what altitude does it sit?
About 2,625 feet (800m) above sea level

How much tea does it produce?
About 11 tons per year

How many workers?
30 workers

What types of tea are produced?
We produce mostly specialty Chinese green teas but also some black teas

Describe your estate?
The Yi Xing Ming Ling Xiang Zhen Tea Garden sits within Yi Xing Jiangsu province and not far from the beautiful Lake Taihu—the third largest freshwater lake in China. The tea is grown on an area of 8,6111 square feet (8,000 square metres so, roughly 2 acres or 0.8 hectares). Our year is focused around the plucking season, which starts on or around April 20–26th every year. We manufacture completely by hand, there is no mechanisation.

What is great about the tea grown in Yi Xing Ming Ling Xiang Zhen Tea Garden and why?
We make very good tea, carefully and closely watching the process from start to finish. The process is very much done by hand, but the weather determines much of the quality of the tea.

Can you describe a typical day on the estate?
All the employees have to work on all the elements of the process. So, the same 30 workers pluck the tea and then work in the factory to process it ahead of selling it.

How have you seen the tea industry change? How have the requirements changed for tea growers?
The tea industry in China is still very traditional, since I have been in the business there have been very little changes and this makes me very happy.

How often do you leave the tea estate?
I spend five days working at the tea garden and then have two days at home; though I'm rarely on vacation but am at home working there.

What's your favorite cup? Do you only drink your own tea?
I only drink Chinese green tea and I think Mao Feng green tea is the best.

How do you drink tea? Do you only drink freshly brewed tea?
I like to drink fresh tea from our tea garden. I brew fresh green tea in a Yixing clay teapot and drink it from a glass cup. I don't like flavored teas but sometimes drink black tea in tea bags. A Yixing clay teapot is made of special zisha clay, which contains various minerals found only in Yixing, China. After several uses the Yixing teapot absorbs tea into its walls and becomes coated; this means it holds onto the flavors of the tea and makes a finer brew. Apparently, there is a rule when using these teapots: never mix the tea— always use the same type of tea in the same teapot.

What do you love about tea?
In short, I love tea. Any good-quality green tea is my favorite; I love the fresh seasonal flavors.

Above Leaf being plucked for Matcha manufacture, Japan.

Opposite Japanese tea bushes are cut by machine and form neat fan-shaped rows.

Who knew?

Call us corny romantics, but we like the story that goes with Mao Feng green tea. It's said that a young man and a beautiful young woman from a tea plantation were in love, but the local tyrant seized her as his concubine. She escaped, only to learn that the tyrant had also killed her lover. Finding his body deep in the mountains she wept and wept until she became the rain, while her lover's body turned into a tea bush. Which is why, according to the legend, the area where Mao Feng green tea grows is cloudy and humid the whole year round. All together now ... aaah!

JAPANESE GREEN TEAS

In stark contrast to the small-scale and worker-based production of tea in China, the Japanese have taken artisan tea making to another level with slick mechanization (see also page 93). They are really the only region in the world that still makes good tea but does not do the processing by hand.

SENCHA
Often just referred to as Japanese green tea, Sencha makes up about 70% of the tea produced in Japan. If you look back at the processing of tea, you'll see that steaming is one of the processes (see page 101). The length of the steam applied to the tea impacts on its taste: a 20-second blast gives a strong aroma and a lighter-colored cup whereas a longer steam (of up to 160 seconds) gives rise to more broken leaf, a darker-colored tea, and a stronger flavor.

GYOKURO
Gyokuro Tamahomare is its full name, but we call it Gyokuro for short. It's grown predominantly in the area around Kyoto (Japan's ancient capital). Gyokuro makes up less than 1% of Japan's tea production but it's one of its most precious teas. What makes this tea so special? Twenty days before the tea leaves are to be picked, the tea bushes are covered with a curtain of meshlike fabric. Covering the bushes in this way forces them to raise their production of chlorophyll (the pigment that makes leaves green) and amino acids. The resulting leaves are supergreen and rich in a particular amino acid—theanine—which gives the tea a particular sweetness, referred to as *ooi-ka* in Japan.

GENMAICHA
What do you put with green tea to make it go further? Toasted and puffed rice, of course! This tea is a teapigs favorite—we call it "popcorn tea" as it has hints of popcorn—and it's made on a Sencha tea base. Made for centuries by the poor of Japan who were trying to eke out their supplies of an expensive commodity (tea) by mixing it with a less-expensive ingredient (rice), it is now a staple drink in Japan. The combination of green tea and sweet, nutty toasted rice is becoming popular around the world.

KUKICHA
When we talk of quality tea and making a tasty brew, we normally refer to the plucking of buds and leaves, never the stem of the bush; but we'll make an exception for this tea. Most commonly Kukicha (also known as Bocha or "twig tea") is a mixture of yellow leaf stems and rich, bright-green Sencha leaf, but it can also be blended with Gyokuro. Some say this tea is like making the best of the leftovers; the resulting tea is a light, not too astringent green tea. And because the stems don't contain as much caffeine as the leaves, Kukicha is a naturally lower-caffeine drink.

HOJICHA
When is a green tea not green? When it's brown, of course! Hojicha translates as "roasted tea" and this roasting helps to standardize the flavors of the tea, most commonly Bancha tea. This distinctly Japanese tea collects together the final teas of the harvesting season and then roasts them in a porcelain pot over a charcoal fire; the resulting tea is woody and nutty.

MATCHA
A SUPERHERO AMONG TEAS

Let us introduce you to Matcha—this superconcentrated green tea is ground to a fine powder and is packed with nutrients. We like to think of Matcha as a superhero in the world of tea.

Genuine Matcha comes from Japan where it has been drunk as a ceremonial beverage by Buddhist monks and royalty for over 900 years. But don't be surprised if you've never heard of it as, until recently, virtually all Matcha has been consumed only within Japan.

Matcha—like all tea—comes from the tea plant, *Camellia sinensis*. What makes Matcha so special is that the leaves are grown under shade for two weeks before picking. This short burst of growth out of direct sunlight causes the leaves to produce lots of amino acids and chlorophyll (the stuff that gives leaves their bright-green color).

Then, the leaves are steamed and then baked slowly to form Tencha. The stems and veins of the leaves are removed to allow for only the pure leaf to go through to production of Matcha. The Tencha leaves are ground to a very fine powder using special granite stones. Once it's ground, the powder is packed and sealed immediately to preserve all of its wonderful nutrients.

MATCHA'S BENEFITS
Why is Matcha so good for you? The secret is in the way it's drunk. When you drink regular green tea, you throw away the leaves; it's a bit

HOW TO DRINK: Matcha, anytime, anywhere

Matcha is incredibly versatile. You can drink it as a hot tea but you can also add it to fruit juices, smoothies, and hot or cold milk (see pages 196, 199, and 200). So it's easy to get your Matcha hit! Whichever way you choose, here's how to make it.

POW

1 Take ½ teaspoon of Matcha.

2 Add it to your chosen liquid—hot or cold water, fruit juice or smoothie, hot or cold milk.

3 Give it a whisk (electric handheld whisks work like a charm) and take a swig!

Because Matcha is a powder, you don't just have to drink it. You can add it to your oatmeal, cereal, or yogurt.

Above Tea leaves growing on a bush, in close up.

like boiling spinach, throwing away the spinach, and just drinking the water—you will get some of the nutrients, but you're throwing away the best bit. With Matcha, you mix the vibrant, nutrient-rich powder into liquid and ingest the whole tea leaf. So, you consume more of that special green tea goodness!

Matcha is believed to give you a slow release of energy that lasts throughout the day while keeping you calm, alert, and focused at the same time. That's why Japanese students drink this wonderful green stuff when they're cramming for their exams and it's also why Buddhist monks drink Matcha to keep them calm and focused during hours of mediation.

Drinking Matcha is like drinking 10 cups of regular green tea for its nutrient value—that's why we call it superpower green tea; we think it gives you bucketfuls of sprightliness.

MATCHA, MATCHA EVERYWHERE

But what we love about Matcha is how versatile it is. As it's a powder, you can add it to almost anything. In Japan, Matcha is used to flavor popcorn, ice cream, cakes (see page 173), and cookies.

Right Louise inspecting green tea bushes, under shade, destined to become Matcha powder.

THE SCIENCEY BITS BEHIND THE BENEFITS

Green tea flavonoids

Matcha contains high amounts of natural green tea flavonoids known as catechins. The major catechin found in Matcha is epigallocatechin gallate, not easy to pronounce but fortunately also known as EGCG. Much of the scientific research into the antioxidant properties of green tea are focussed on how EGCG works within the human body.

Brain power

A Japanese study in 1992 also found that an important amino acid called L-theanine can help improve learning performance, promote concentration, and support the immune system.

Slow-release energy

As with all green teas, Matcha contains caffeine, a natural stimulant, as well as the amino acid L-theanine. These two compounds appear to work together to give a slow release of energy; many Matcha drinkers report that they feel alert and focused for many hours. Much research is being conducted into how L-theanine may help promote alpha brain waves. The good news is that high-grade Matcha contains even more

L-theanine as it has been grown in the shade for longer, which boosts the production of this important amino acid.

Healthy skin

Green tea contains polyphenols, this may not mean much to you and us, but the clever people at the University of Alabama have found that consumption of green tea polyphenols can inhibit UV-radiation-induced skin damage. It is well known that the sun's UV rays can damage skin, cause premature aging, and even cause skin cancer. Their study found that these polyphenols can be used to prevent sun-induced skin disorders, helping to keep your skin young and beautiful.

Calorie burning

A lot of scientific studies are looking at the effect that green tea may have on the body's thermogenesis (that is, the rate it burns calories) and on its impact upon fat oxidization during exercise. There are no conclusive clinical studies but green tea extract is now used in many slimming supplements. Matcha is probably the purest form of green tea extract—and, what's more, it's lovely to drink.

meet the tea maker

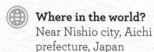

Louise meets … Mr. Yoshio Sugita, a Japanese Matcha producer, who says that Matcha "is one of the most unique and valuable teas in the world." His company, Aiya, based in Nishio, Aichi, Japan, has been producing Matcha since 1888 and sells Matcha worldwide.

Where in the world?
Near Nishio city, Aichi prefecture, Japan

At what altitude does it sit?
Over 1,970 feet (600m) above sea level

How much tea does it produce? 1,323 tons per year of Matcha

How many workers?
150 full-time workers

What types of tea are produced?
Japanese Matcha

What got you into tea?
My family has been in the world of tea for 12 years. I was born into the business and learned everything about growing, processing, and making tea from an early age.

How have you seen the tea industry change? How have the requirements changed for tea growers?
From our point of view, we see Matcha not as a tea, but as a food, because you consume the whole leaf. Accordingly, Matcha is a popular ingredient in different food products throughout Asia. I believe that soon Matcha will become equally accepted in Europe and in the United States of America as a unique flavor and ingredient.

What manufacturing processes do you use at your estate?
Matcha is made from Tencha tea leaves. Tencha is a green tea that is grown under shade, and which is then steamed and baked before being ground into powder. Our Matcha is made by grinding only the flesh of tea leaves, no stalks are included. The grinding takes places in what's known as a cleanroom, where the temperature and humidity are carefully controlled and the air is filtered. The tea leaves are ground to an incredibly fine size—an average grain of Matcha powder will measure just 5–10 microns across (that's 1 millionth of a meter!) and it will take one grinding machine (still using granite) an hour to produce a single 1¼ ounces (30g) tin.

How do you drink tea? Do you only drink freshly brewed tea?
I like to drink pure green tea from a tea bowl and never ever use tea bags. Quality is an essential requirement in the tea I drink.

What's your favorite cup?
I drink one bowl of Matcha three times a day.

What do you love about tea?
I believe that tea is a product that is not only good for the health but also has no negative associations. In my opinion, Japanese green tea is an all-round good product. Japanese green tea provides tea farmers in Japan with a sustainable and fair income base. The product itself is delicious, as well as having a high nutritional value.

Opposite Tencha leaf pre-grinding..

This page Ground Matcha powder, about to be made into tea in the traditional way.

OOLONG TEA

Tea or not tea? It's tea as it comes from the *Camellia sinensis* plant
Where is it grown? Guangdong and Fujian provinces and Taiwan, China
How does it taste? From rich and fruity to floral and delicate
How to make? Brew for 3 minutes
How to serve? Hot without milk
What makes it special? Its style of manufacture

Oolong (also known as wulong) is a style of manufacture that originates from China (Guangdong and Fujian provinces) but is also huge in Taiwan; nowadays Taiwan tea growers almost exclusively grow oolong tea. We always describe oolong tea as being "between black and green," which sums up its character: a combination of the flavor of green tea and the strength of black tea.

In contrast to white teas, oolong teas' flavors range from woody dark to very light and floral. The leaves are oxidized and rolled to different degrees to give distinctly different flavors—the percentage of oxidation varies from 10% (closer to green tea) to 70% (closer to black tea). China tends to produce the darker, heavier oolongs. See what processing goes on for oolong in The journey of a tea leaf, pages 98–103.

Nick always says it is wrong to have a favorite tea, that it is like having a favorite child. That said, oolong is my favorite tea. We'd like to share a couple of our fave oolongs with you: Tung Ting and Li Shan.

TUNG TING

Also known as Dong Ding and translates as "frozen peaks," this oolong tea is grown in the Nantou region in the center of the island of Taiwan and is harvested four times a year (April, June, September, and November). The Nantou area produces more than half of Taiwan's oolong tea. The quality can be a bit mixed, but the Tung Ting mountainous region produces some really yummy teas. The leaves are rolled really, really tightly, and the resulting flavor is sweet and very floral. The depth of flavor is long lasting and so the leaves can easily be reinfused several times.

LI SHAN

Grown in the Taichung region in Taiwan, the Li Shan mountain offers a high-altitude growing area for tea at 6,500 feet (1,980m) above sea level; Li Shan translates as "pear mountain" as this area is full of pear, peach, and apple orchards. There, the tea grows very slowly and so is harvested only twice per year (May and October); compared with the Tung Ting's quarterly harvests. The taste is heavenly—one of spring flowers, with a rich creamy flavor.

Left Top-notch oolong tea.

Meet the tea maker

Louise meets … Lim Ying Jiu who grows oolong tea. His estate is a 30-minute walk from the nearest town-Yuchi, which sits right on Sun Moon Lake, the largest lake in Taiwan. He has two farms: the smaller one is a 5-acre (2-hectare) organic farm; the larger one measures 15 acres (6 hectares), is mountainous and is not yet certified organic.

 Where in the world?
Near the Sun Moon Lake in Taiwan

 At what altitude does it sit?
The smaller organic farm sits about 984 feet (300m) above sea level, while the larger mountainous farm is about 3,600 feet (1,100m)

 How much tea does it produce?
It varies with each season

 How many workers?
Most of the year only three or four of us, but up to 50 during harvest

 What types of tea are produced?
Tung Ting oolong and Gong Fu black tea (it's a ruby tea due to the cross of tea bushes used)

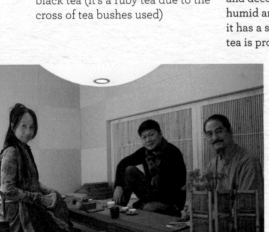

Describe your estate?
My estate is in the mountains. The area around it is green and picturesque; from the top of the estate you can see Sun Moon Lake. I have plans for expansion too.

What got you into tea?
My family have been growing oolong tea for a number of years, so four years ago I decided to start growing tea myself. I was mentored by Master Aoenes, a tea master made famous for popularizing black tea in Taiwan. We experiment with different production methods and new tea varieties.

What is great about the tea grown in Taiwan and why?
I use an organic microbe fertilizer, which breaks down organic material into a more usable form for the plants, and it also treats and decomposes the soil. The air here is humid and hot and there's lots of rain. So, it has a similar climate to where Assam tea is produced in India. However, due to the combination of Assam and Taiwanese bushes, the tea is a brighter reddish color.

How have you seen the tea industry change?
The tea industry in Taiwan has traditionally been export-orientated, but now there is rising global competition and tea exports from Taiwan have been declining. The costs of growing tea is increasing for a number of reasons, and it's harder than ever to find young tea workers. Tea is a tea grower's life, though, so we have to face the difficulties.

What manufacturing processes do you use at your estate?
I use mostly orthodox methods, though I have started to introduce more innovative methods, such as using aerodynamics for tea withering. My factory is a small-scale family factory, because I love quality tea.

Can you describe a typical day on the estate?
If it's not harvest season there's not much work to be done. I only need to visit the farm three times a day to water the leaves and do some weeding. During the plucking season, I'll have 30 to 40 extra staff to help pluck the leaves and a further four to eight people to help process the tea. The pluckers start at 7 a.m. and work until 3 p.m., unless it is raining in which case they can't work. We harvest between 2,200 and 2,645 pounds (1,000–1,200kg) of tea per day. The tea processing begins as soon as the first batch of leaves is in, usually 8 a.m. and carries on until 6 p.m. the next day. Withering tea leaves takes 12 to 16 hours and twisting the tea takes 10 to 12 hours. To give you an idea, 11 pounds (5kg) of leaves gives us 2¼ pounds (1kg) of tea. This process goes on for about seven or eight days, which can get really tiring.

How often do you leave the tea estate?
I spend most of my time on the farm. It's a full-time job, so I don't ever go on vacation.

What's your favorite cup? Do you only drink your own tea?
My favorite tea is my own Sun Moon Lake Black Ruby tea. I usually drink my own but sometimes try out others.

How do you drink tea?
I like to drink tea slowly, anytime and anywhere. I sometimes like to drink "riper" (fermented) teas, too.

What do you love about tea?
I love tea for its delicate, mild, dainty, and fresh tastes. I also love it for its calming nature and Zen quality.

PU-ERH TEA

Tea or not tea? It's tea as it comes from the *Camellia sinensis* plant
Where is it grown? Pu-erh, China
How does it taste? Earthy, strong, and smooth
How to make? Brew for 3 minutes
How to serve? Hot without milk
What makes it special? Its history and its superslow fermentation

Pu-erh is one of the oldest forms of Chinese tea; its use can be traced as far back as the Tang dynasty (618–907). This tea takes its name from the town of Pu-erh in Yunnan province in southwestern China. Pu-erh became the hub of tea trading and all the tea traded there took its name, whatever they were.

Back then, transport was mostly via horse, so the tea had to be packaged in a suitable form and processed to be able to deal with long journeys. The locals of Pu-erh town created a particular way of processing the tea so that it actually improved, rather than deteriorated, with age: they compressed them into "cakes" (pictured left), which slowly oxidize over time. It's not the tea for impatient people since the best pu-erh tea takes at least 30 years to come to maturity; although fermentation (aka oxidation) can take anytime between 10 and 50 years.

The cultivar grown for pu-erh tea is the Yunnan Da Ye and it's typically harvested in April from the mountains neighboring Pu-erh town.

> **Tea tempers the spirits and harmonizes the mind, dispels lassitude and relieves fatigue, awakens thought and prevents drowsiness, lightens or refreshes the body, and clears the perceptive faculties.**
>
> Lu Yu, *Classic of Tea: Origins and Rituals*

Above An array of pu-erh cakes wrapped up and stacked in piles.

Opposite An unwrapped cake of pu-erh tea.

RAW OR COOKED?

No, we're not talking steak here or even sashimi, but tea. There was a huge demand for pu-erh tea but, because of the superslow fermentation process, it was expensive, and in short supply. So, those in the Chinese tea industry developed a new kind of pu-erh called "shou pu-erh"; "shou" translates literally as "cooked." To define the original kind, it was given the name "sheng" or "raw." Unlike the sheng's 10 to 50 years of fermentation, the shou pu-erh could be ready in 45 to 60 days; it was designed to be drunk straightaway (no waiting around for years with this brew) to fulfill the desires of all those people demanding pu-erh tea! Now, that's what we call fast.

For pu-erh teas, the leaves are processed as for a green tea (see page 98) but they are not completed with a firing. Instead, the teas are left to age and develop, fermenting very slowly. As we mentioned earlier:
• sheng pu-erh continues to age at home; this one gets better with time
• shou pu-erh are dried to halt the fermentation and can be drunk immediately.

Before the leaves are compressed into a "cake," traditionally a piece of paper with a trademark or *nei fei* is popped on top just before the tea is compressed. The trademark contains the information about where the tea was grown and processed. And the shapes of "cake" are not just round, flat cakes—though those do have some lucky Chinese symbolism—but they can be compressed into all manner of shapes, from a brick to a nest to a mushroom or even a pig! Pu-erh is a traditional (read, expensive) gift.

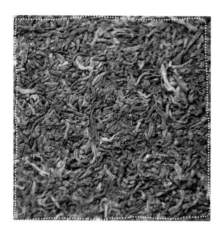

BLACK TEA

Tea or not tea? It's tea as it comes from the *Camellia sinensis* plant
Where is it grown? India, Sri Lanka, China, and Africa
How does it taste? Aromatic, strong, and full of flavor
How to make? Brew for 3 minutes
How to serve? Hot with or without milk; iced with lemon (and sugar!)
What makes it special? Its level of fermentation; it's fully fermented

In Britain, black tea is so "regular" that it is often referred to as normal tea—shame on us because the reality is it can be far from normal; the Chinese, by the way, call this tea *Hong cha* or red tea. Black tea (as we learned earlier, see pages 98–103) is fully fermented. The big differences in types of black tea relate to its method of processing—whether it follows the orthodox route or the CTC (cut, tear, curl) route (see page 100). Orthodox processing keeps the leaves larger and twisted and allows for more complex and delicate flavors in the tea, whereas CTC leaves are smaller and round, giving a stronger color and flavor to a brew.

The big players in black tea are East Africa and Southern Asia. Within those regions there are areas that produce very different styles of black tea, for example in India—Darjeeling and Assam. Another big producer is Argentina, where they produce a clean, very black leaf tea, which tends to be used in the US for iced tea due to its clear light liquor and simple flavor.

In the world of black tea, the production process can be fast and slick—for instance, plucking to sorting can all be done within one day. While a factory may be automated, the art of good tea making is still down to a team of knowledgeable experts. And the tea world has its fair share of these. There are many regional (and local) specific styles of manufacture, which are handed down the generations of tea masters!

THE VERY BASICS OF TEA GRADING

Here's how we start to describe black tea.

BROKEN (B, FOR SHORT)
bigger leaf, broken or cut found in various sizes and used mainly in loose-leaf tea

FANNINGS (F, FOR SHORT)
medium leaf, small particles of tea leaves (1mm in size) used mainly in tea bags

DUST (D, FOR SHORT)
small leaf for intense brewing, only used in tea bags

GET THE BASICS OF TEA GRADING

When it comes to tea there's so many grades—from top-notch large leaf pieces with light color to dusty particles with strong, dark colors—the tea industry have created a language of their own to summarize the different types. The language is not universal and very much varies by region. But, in the box on the right we share the very basics of the vocabulary used for grading black tea, whether its processed using the orthodox route or via CTC.

Opposite Sacks of black tea awaiting onward transport from the Melfort Tea Factory, Nuwara-Eliya region, Sri Lanka.

TEA GEEK SPEAK

If you want to impress someone with your tea knowledge, try something along the lines of "I only drink 'TGFOP,'" meaning a tippy, golden, flowery, orange pekoe. The lingo used for CTC tea is a little bit more straightforward (see below) than that for orthodox teas (see opposite). Here are our highlights.

Top of the pile (what are known as primary grades) for CTC teas:

Broken Pekoe 1

Forms about 12 to 14% of the total production and has the largest size particles. Liquors are light in color but have a strong flavor.

Pekoe Fannings 1

Forms the bulk of the production (about 58 to 60%); it's made up of black grainy particles slightly smaller than the BP1.

Pekoe Dust

Forms 10 to 12% of the production; it's often black and finer than the PF1 with thick liquors and aroma.

Dust 1

Forms about 4 to 6% of the production; it is made up of the smallest particles and characterized by strong liquors.

Bottom of the bunch (what are known as secondary grades):

Dust
Made up of tiny bits of broken leaf often used to brew strong tea.

Broken Mixed Fannings (some call this "mattress fiber" instead as that's what it looks like!)
Fibrous bits with very little trace of black teas.

LET'S TALK ORTHODOX BLACK TEAS

As with CTC processed teas, tea industry bods use a series of acronyms to describe the quality and character of different black teas that follow orthodox processing; it tends to be Asian or Indian black teas that follow the orthodox route. So, if you're keen to know what's good—broadly speaking, more letters mean more fancy—although some great smaller leaf teas can be found.

Say it "peck-oh" or "pee-koh." This Chinese term means "white down" and refers to the character of the young leaves. Pekoe and Orange Pekoe are terms for the grade of tea.

Smaller leaf, broken or cut.

GFBOP
Golden Flowery Broken Orange (Pekoe)
Produced mainly in Assam

GBOP
Golden (Broken) Orange Pekoe
The next, second sorting with few tips

BP AND OP
Broken Pekoe and Orange Pekoe
A brown to black, heavily broken tea from Indonesia, Ceylon, and Southern India; often with very woody, stalky particles

GFOP
Golden Flowery Orange Pekoe
The top grade from the only surviving Kenya tea garden that manufactures tippy tea

BOP
Broken Orange Pekoe
A uniform dense leaf that gives a quickly colored infusion. The main broken grade of Ceylon, South India, Java, and China

TGBOP
Tippy Golden Broken Orange Pekoe
The finest broken grade produced in Darjeeling and Assam. Highly tippy

FOP
Flowery Orange Pekoe
Plain grade of Indian leaf tea

BPS
Broken Pekoe Souchong
Assam and Darjeeling, pearl-shaped leaves

FBOP
Flowery Broken Orange Pekoe
A coarser broken grade with some tips, it comes from Assam, Indonesia, China, and Bangladesh

OP SUP
Orange Pekoe (Superior)
Bit Tippy. Produced mainly in Indonesia

TGFOP
(Tippy) Golden Flowery Orange Pekoe
Seen mainly in Darjeeling and Assam

TIPPY
Only produced in Indonesia

SFTGFOP1
Special Finest Tippy Golden Flowery Orange Pekoe 1
Super duper grade of tea

FTGFOP1
Finest Tippy Golden Flowery Orange Pekoe 1
Mainly from Darjeeling, some from Assam. Top grade tea

Well, that's normal English, not tea geek-speak.

The lighter, or golden, tips of the tea (leaf tips of the young, tender tea leaf bud) that do not affect the color in the cup.

Who knew?
The word "orange" in Orange Pekoe doesn't describe the color of the leaf (that would be strange) but, in fact, refers to the Dutch royal family who were among the first to import tea into Europe.

INDIAN TEA

The three biggest-producing regions of black tea in India are two you've most probably heard of: Darjeeling and Assam and, another that you are less likely to have heard of, Nilgiri Mountains.

DARJEELING

All around the hilltown of Darjeeling are blankets of green and gentle slopes of some 80-odd tea gardens and estates, stretching off into the distance. It's high up, too—over 6,800 feet (2,000m)—and the regular mists rise to reveal the most spectacular vistas of the mountains all around; Darjeeling in West Bengal, India, sits at the feet of the Himalayas.

The extreme positioning of the tea bushes, the altitude, the cool weather, and the expert production methods all come together to produce what is an amazing range of teas. Darjeeling is home to some of the best teas in the world. We like to think of Darjeeling as the champagne of teas. In fact, its status is recognized now (just like French champagne is the world over) and only teas originating in Darjeeling can take the name Darjeeling.

Teas at Darjeeling range from black and brown leaf with a strong flavor to pale-green leaf with a light, golden taste; whichever you like, we think they're both best drunk without milk. Darjeelings are known for having a muscatel character—if you're a fan of floral dessert wine then find a Darjeeling to match.

HARVESTS: Darjeeling flush

There are four harvests in Darjeeling giving rise to teas of different characters and tastes. The flush refers to the growth spurt the tea leaves go through before a harvest.

1 FIRST FLUSH (FIRST PICKING SEASON) IN MID-MARCH–END APRIL/MAY.
The taste/appearance: astringent and sharper tasting. The bushes have been dormant over the winter and the shoots are supertender. They have a green/black appearance.

2 SECOND FLUSH IN MAY–JUNE.
The taste/appearance: rapid growth gives a stronger, sweeter taste. This harvest is where you will really taste muscatel.

3 MONSOON HARVEST IN JULY–OCTOBER.
The taste/appearance: the heavy rain means rapid growth but weakens the strength and complexity of the flavors.

4 FALL FLUSH IN OCTOBER–NOVEMBER.
The taste/appearance: less rain and cooler weather slows the production and the first flush characteristics appear.

Meet the tea maker

Louise meets … Sanjay Bansal, who was born into tea and is now chairman of the Ambootia group, which owns the Happy Valley Tea Estate. Nestled amid the wispy clouds straddling the eastern slopes of the majestic Himalayas lies a valley–Happy Valley, and the only tea garden in Darjeeling town.

Where in the world?
Darjeeling, West Bengal, India

At what altitude does it sit?
6,800 feet (2,070m)

How much tea does it produce?
44 tons

How many workers?
276

What types of tea are produced?
Orthodox black, green, white, and specialty teas

Opposite, top The tea harvest at Happy Valley; soon to become Darjeeling tea.

Opposite bottom The withering room at Happy Valley.

Below A view from on high, looking down the valley.

Describe your estate?

Happy Valley is located in Darjeeling town and, therefore, has easy access to all facilities. It is about 3 hours' drive from the airport and the railroad station.

From Happy Valley estate you get a panoramic view of Darjeeling from its altitude of over 6,800 feet (2,000m), occupying a sprawling 438 acres (177 hectares) of dense underbrush and forest cover. The unique geographical combination of altitude, soil, and climate makes the tea here have a distinct flavor. With the glorious Kanchenjunga bearing down upon it, its vantage point allows a mesmerising view of the quaint little township of Darjeeling.

This tea estate has quite a history. David Wilson, an Englishman, established the tea estate in 1854 as Wilson Tea Estate. By early 1860, the garden had started production. In 1903, an Indian Sahib by the name of Tarapada Banerjee took over the estate and later, in 1929, merged it with another nearby estate he bought; thus was formed Happy Valley Tea Estate. Regrettably however, the garden fell into bad times and the owners abandoned it. Sadly, Happy Valley Tea Estate was declared sick and abandoned around 2000.

Notwithstanding the salubrious climatic conditions, Happy Valley remained predominantly unproductive for many years. It was subject to identical impediments that plague tea gardens all over the country—poor management and labor disputes that teetered on the brink of violence.

In March 2007, the management was taken over by us. Subsequently we implemented good agriculture and manufacturing practices. We follow an organic and biodynamic system of agriculture as well as following international standards for quality and food safety.

What got you into tea?

I was born on the nearby Ambootia Tea Estate. I am a third-generation tea worker; tea runs through my blood.

What is great about the tea grown on Happy Valley Tea Estate and why?

To me every aspect of tea is great. Darjeeling tea forms a very important part of India's cultural and collective intellectual heritage. It is of considerable importance to the economy of India because of its international reputation.

Darjeeling tea cannot be grown or manufactured anywhere else in the world. The quality, reputation and characteristics of Darjeeling tea are essentially attributable to its geographical origin. It is one of India's treasured "geographical indication" products. Only tea grown and produced in the defined area of the Darjeeling district in the state of West Bengal, India can be called Darjeeling tea.

On November 9, 2011, Darjeeling tea became the first Indian product to be protected as a geographical indication in the EU. Darjeeling tea is now legally recognized and protected in India and in the EU. This registration of Darjeeling tea is the ultimate protection of the rights of the discerning consumers, which will in turn ensure the availability of authentic Darjeeling tea.

Darjeeling tea has a unique flavor that cannot be replicated anywhere else. It is referred to as "The Queen of Teas" and its golden brew is light and bright in color.

How have you seen the tea industry change? How have the requirements changed for tea growers?

The tea industry focus has been to improve the quality of tea. We've listened to consumers and they are more aware of quality as an issue. We feel that good-quality teas receive a premium, whereas no consumer wants poor-quality tea.

What manufacturing processes do you use at your estate?

At Happy Valley we produce orthodox black, green, white, and specialty teas (see page 100 for more information on orthodox processing).

Can you describe a typical day on the estate?

The work at the tea estate starts early; on my visits I arrive at 6 a.m. and I walk around the factory for 30 minutes to get an idea of how the previous day's harvest is getting on. After the factory visit, I walk off into the fields. I'll find just the right spot and eat my breakfast in the outdoors and will wander around the fields until lunchtime, about 1 p.m. After lunch I return to the factory to taste the teas that have been processed that morning—this is our quality control. Next, I'll visit the factory's withering area to assess the quality of the green leaf there. Some time after 5 p.m. I'll sit down with the management of the estate to discuss the current workload and also what's coming up.

How often do you leave the tea estate?

I am stationed at the tea company's head office in Kolkata, but visit the plantation every two months to provide my inputs into the field work and manufacturing to fine tune the processes for a superlative quality. The tea estate is managed by a team comprising of a manager, assistant managers, staff, and supervisors.

What's your favorite cup? Do you only drink your own tea?

Tea made in every season becomes my favorite—as each season produces teas with different characters and flavors. Yes, I am addicted to the tea we produce—as I think we produce the best tea.

How do you drink tea? Do you only drink freshly brewed tea?

I drink tea throughout the day and when not traveling I brew loose-leaf tea that is fresh from the season. However, I do keep a stock of my favorites to be savored in the cold months when there is no harvest.

What do you love about tea?

I love the passion behind all aspects of growing and producing tea.

ASSAM

In stark contrast to the high-altitude mountainside tea estates in Darjeeling, the beautiful region of Assam in northeastern India (near Bangladesh and Myanmar) is close to sea level, with a warm climate and heavy rainfall. In India both cultivars of tea grow but each thrives in different locations. Over time, growers have discovered that *Camellia sinensis* var. *sinensis* cultivars grow best at high altitudes while *Camellia sinensis* var. *assamica* bushes flourish in the plains, or at a slightly lower altitude of 1,000 feet (300m). And, lest we forget to say, Assam is also home to five national parks and the one-horned rhino!

Here, tea is grown predominantly in the valley either side of the Brahmaputra river. Assam has about 800 tea estates and is the largest tea-producing region in the world. The low altitude, heavy rainfall, and rich soil all contribute to excellent cropping conditions. The varietal grown here is *Camellia sinensis* var. *assamica* (see also page 90). This larger, tougher-leaf varietal is used to produce both CTC and orthodox teas (see page 100). Both the CTC and the orthodox teas from Assam are drunk in India and sold all over the world.

The finest orthodox Assam teas are incredibly popular; they give malty complex flavors. The character of a CTC Assam tea is strong and bold and also malty. What we call the "thickness in the mouth" (see also page 144) of CTC Assam teas, in particular, is an integral part of "the great British cuppa." Brits (whether we know it or not) love the strong, malty, thick character that Assam teas give. At teapigs, we use it in our Everyday Brew to compliment the flavor and briskness given by the other teas in that blend.

Who knew?

Before the 1950s the people of India hardly drank tea, but now they drink almost 80% of the tea grown in India, mostly Assam and Darjeeling!

Nilgiri Mountains

The Nilgiri Mountains, or Blue Mountains, lie at the southwestern tip of India and 60,000 acres (24,280 hectares) of this area are dedicated to tea production; it's the third biggest tea-growing region in India. In tea terms the Nilgiri region is lucky (some would say unlucky) as it has two rainy seasons. All this rain means the tea grows year round, so the harvest can be year round too.

The quality of Nilgiri tea ranges from some of the finest examples of high-altitude, small production teas that have a delicate flavor to much more regular-quality base teas used for blending.

Below Bundles of freshly plucked leaves being carried by the tea pluckers.

meet the tea maker

Louise meets … Mr. Hegde of Korakundah Tea. Korakundah is the highest tea-growing area in India, possibly the world. And with its sister tea estate (Chamraj), it is the largest manufacturer-exporter estate group in the Nilgiri Mountains.

Where in the world?
Nilgiri Mountains, Tamil Nadu, Southern India

At what altitude does it sit?
About 7,500 to 8,000 feet (2,285 to 2,440m) above sea level

How much tea does it produce?
661 tons per year

How many workers?
350

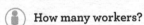
What types of tea are produced?
Organic green, oolong, and chamomile teas

Describe your estate?
Korakundah Organic is part of the United Nilgiri Tea Estates Company Limited and has its 93-year-old plantations situated in the Blue Mountains of the Nilgiris. It sits between two tiger reserves. The South Indian hills and weather pattern gives Korakundah tea it's special exotic flavor. Korakundah also is the highest tea growing area in India, possibly the world.

What got you into tea?
I've been working at the estate for 39 years and still enjoy everything about the estate and tea.

How have you seen the tea industry change? How have the requirements changed for tea growers?
The machinery has changed over the years to comply with the FSSAI regulations and also the consumption of tea has changed because of younger generations choosing tea over other beverages. Organic tea is in great demand in the international market.

What manufacturing processes do you use at your estate?
At Korakundah, we are organic and follow the orthodox method of processing for our green and black teas.

Can you describe a typical day on the estate?
A day on the estate usually starts with tasting the previous day's manufacture and visiting the bushes and looking into day-to-day activities.

What's your favorite cup?
Frost tea, I love its muscatel taste.

How do you drink tea? Do you only drink freshly brewed tea?
I brew tea in a pot, mostly green tea, and always go for quality.

What do you love about tea?
Seeing a plant growing in a unique location being sent all over the world to be enjoyed by many.

SRI LANKA

Not long ago, this island in the Indian Ocean (officially known as the Democratic Socialist Republic of Sri Lanka) didn't have any tea bushes on it whatsoever; instead, it was covered in coffee plantations. But from the late 19th century (for several reasons), Sri Lanka made the switch from coffee to tea, and its tea production has never looked back; Sri Lanka is the one of the big five tea producers in the world (see page 96). The teas grown here are known as Ceylon teas, as Ceylon was how Sri Lanka was formerly known and that's a term that's stuck in the tea trade to the present day.

SRI LANKAN TEA GROWING—LOW TO HIGH

Its tropical climate means that several tea harvests are possible every year and the tea gardens or estates span all parts and levels of the island. Very broadly speaking, you can categorize the black teas of Sri Lanka by altitude:

As you'd expect, the flavor and character of the teas grown at different levels are also different:

High-grown teas
(from 3,940 to 6,560 feet/1,200 to 2,000m)

High-grown teas
are prized for their superdelicate citrus notes.

Midgrown teas
(from 1,970 to 3,940 feet/ 600 to 1,200m)

Midgrown teas
are full bodied with a medium flavor.

Low-grown teas
(up to 600m/ 1,970ft)

Low-grown teas
produce a strong character with a very wiry black leaf.

KENYA AND TANZANIA

Their equatorial climates allow tea growing—and hence harvesting—all year round.

The tea-growing region sits west of Nairobi, predominantly around Kericho but stretching up toward the Rift Valley. This area of high, rolling and lush hills are where most tea gardens are situated (between 5,000 and 6,500 feet/1,500–2,000m) and sits in contrast to the dry north of the country. Kenyan tea growers are broadly either small farmers who work under an umbrella organization called the Kenyan Tea Development Agency (who sells the tea on their behalf) or large-scale producers owning a number of estates. Kenya is one of the top five tea-growing nations in the world—tea is harvested year round—and exports over 90% of its production.

Kenya produces bright yellow brisk teas as well as rich, red, coppery teas.

MALAWI

We think Malawi has to be one of the most beautiful tea-growing countries in the world. The tea-growing region is sparsely populated and sits at the base of Mount Mulanje. Mostly, tea is grown and processed by independent producers who also own factories. Tea harvests happen from October to April —that's their summertime.

Malawian teas tend to be thin and very red (think, tomato soup!). Much of the harvests are exported for use in tea blends for large European companies.

RWANDA AND BURUNDI -

Rwandan tea is planted at high altitudes (6,235 to 8,200 feet/1,900–2,500m) and on well-drained marshes (5,085 to 5,905 feet/1,550–1,800m). Tea is grown on 11 estates.

Teas grown on the mountainsides of Rwanda and Burundi are bright and brisk; they are not widely available as single-estate teas but they are well worth seeking out.

In Burundi, tea is the second-largest cash crop after coffee and 80% of tea comes from village plantations. Here, tea is harvested throughout the year and provides about 60,000 households with a regular source of income.

AFRICAN TEA

Although some tea producers in Africa have been growing tea for over a century, the tea industry generally views them as relative newbies in the production of black tea. Most tea growers in African countries use the *Camellia sinensis* var. *assamica* cultivar as it best suits their subtropical climates. Huge corporations tend to dominate and own acres and acres of tea estates and operate on a volume basis. In terms of growing tea, the key African producers are all in the east of Africa, as the climate of the great lakes region suits the growing of tea: Kenya, Malawi, Tanzania, Burundi, Rwanda, Uganda, and Mozambique who use predominantly the CTC tea production route (see also page 100). As well as black tea, rooibos is also grown in South Africa; though that's not a true tea, strictly speaking.

Above Tea workers walking through the Mount Mulanje area, Malawi.

meet the tea maker

Louise meets ... Amar Pal Singh Shaw from the Pfunda Tea Estate-one of the leading tea estates in Rwanda, Africa. Pfunda lies below the Nyiragongo volcano, one of the volcanoes forming the Virunga Massif, which is home to mountain gorillas, and above Lake Kivu, in an area known as the Congo-Nile Crest, in the Western Province of Rwanda.

 Where in the world?
Western Rwanda, Africa

 At what altitude does it sit?
From 5,577 to 7,218 feet (1,700–2,200m) above sea level

 How much tea does it produce?
2,590 tons per year

 How many workers?
A total of 2,342, fairly evenly split between men and women

What types of tea are produced?
Single estate black tea

Describe your estate?
Pfunda Tea Estate lies a three-hour journey from Kigali: the road meanders along valleys, up hillsides, atop ridges, and climbs over crests, bringing into view numerous hill ranges, the hillsides covered with "patchwork quilt" fields; every inch of land is farmed.

What got you into tea?
I grew up among the tea bushes of the Darjeeling district in Northern India, my family had a tea-processing equipment manufacturing and maintenance business there. Tea was a way of life and not an occupation or a job. Me and my wife and children and now grandchildren enjoy the outdoors and free open country, we feel very claustrophobic in a city or urban environment. I've now worked at Pfunda for over 10 years.

How have you seen the tea industry change? How have the requirements changed for tea growers?
In my opinion, there has been no serious change in the tea industry.

What manufacturing processes do you use at your estate?
Pfunda produces quality CTC tea. The process is very simple but needs close monitoring; we ensure that withering takes between 12 and 16 hours; the leaves are cut by rotorvane and CTC; and we ferment/oxidize for 80 to 90 minutes depending on the ambient temperature.

Can you describe a typical day on the estate?
At 5 a.m., the factory starts manufacturing. I arrive about 7 a.m. and go to the office to check the previous day's record books. About 8 o'clock, I taste some tea and take a tour of the factory, discuss factory works with the relevant department heads—tea making, maintenance, and progress on factory expansion projects. At 9 a.m., I go home for breakfast but by 9.30 a.m. I'll be out in the tea fields. About 1.30 p.m., I go back home for some lunch and return again to the office about 3 p.m. At 4.30 p.m., I close the shop and go home.

What's your favorite cup?
Pfunda tea, factory fresh.

How do you drink tea? Do you only drink freshly brewed tea?
Originally hailing from a farming community of Jat Sikhs from the Punjab, I like my tea to be thick, boiled in water with milk, and some cardamom and ginger for added flavor. I am aware that this method of brewing tea is not appreciated by the more discerning tea connoisseur, but I love it.

What do you love about tea?
Tea is my life, I know no other.

HERBAL TEAS

The rule is a simple one: if it's tea, it must come from the *Camellia sinensis* plant. So, what of peppermint tea or chamomile tea? Well, strictly speaking, they're not tea at all, but infusions or, for the truly pedantic, tisanes.

ROOIBOS TEA

The bushmen of Africa have been drinking rooibos (we say "roy-boss") for hundreds of years and they seem to live long and happy lives. The name "rooibos" means red bush, as it's also known, but the red color of this tea comes only from the fermentation process—the rooibos bush is actually green, just like the tea bush.

This soothing drink is sweet and nutty in taste, is naturally caffeine-free, and is low in tannins. As we mentioned before (see page 51), the tea is made from the leaves of the rooibos plant, which grows in just one place— the Cederberg region, deep in the heart of South Africa.

Making rooibos your cup of choice is thought to ease headaches, nervous tension, and insomnia. Rooibos also contains phenylpyretic acid, which is thought to help skin conditions such as eczema. And it's packed with micronutrients, including copper, iron, potassium, calcium, fluoride, zinc, manganese, and alpha-hydroxy acids (yes, the ones in beauty products).

LICORICE

The roots of the small licorice plant, also known as sweet root, can extend to 30 feet (9m) long and it grows throughout Europe and Asia. It is this root that is used to make tea.

CHAMOMILE

Chamomile is one of the old favorites among garden herbs and its reputation as a medicinal plant that makes you snooze is well known. The fresh plant has a lovely scent, with a distinct "appley" smell— not lost on the Greeks, who named it "ground-apple" (Kamal-melon). There are many reputed benefits of drinking chamomile. It is believed to strengthen the immune system, aid digestion, calm nerves, and ease stomach pains.

HONEYBUSH

Like rooibos or red bush, honeybush is another South African wonder bush and, unsurprisingly, is slightly sweeter in taste than rooibos. The name comes from its scented yellow flowers with their distinctly honey scent. According to tradition, the best tea is harvested during its flowering period. Honeybush tea is packed with vitamin C, potassium, calcium, and magnesium. It has a very low tannin content and contains no caffeine whatsoever.

LEMONGRASS

Lemongrass is not just for making fragrant curries it makes an awesome tea. You might well have bought the odd one or two for cooking, but this perennial tufted grass, with its long, sharp-edged blades, grows in dense clumps in tropical or subtropical climates. The plants last three to four years and are harvested every three to five months. Lemongrass is grown throughout South East Asia, Southern India, Sri Lanka, Central Africa, Brazil, Guatemala, the US, and the West Indies.

Its herbal properties are centuries old and are commonly used in Indonesia and Malaysia by herbalists. It seems that lemongrass is a tonic to combat depression and bad moods and to fight fever.

YERBA MATE

Yerba mate is a small evergreen tree or shrub of the holly family, native to the subtropical highlands of northern Argentina, Paraguay, Uruguay, and southern Brazil. It is actually pronounced "yerba mat-hey" but we don't mind if you call it mate—old buddy, old chum.

The word yerba is a corruption of *hierba*, the Spanish for herb, and mate is from a Quechua Indian word *mati* meaning cup. So, you put them together and yerba mate literally means a "cup of herbs."

The Guarani Indians were the first to cure all ills by drinking yerba mate; it is thought to boost immunity, cleanse, and detoxify the blood, combat fatigue, control the appetite, reduce stress, and eliminate insomnia.

Although it can be drunk as an infusion (a tea bag in a cup, aka a *cocido*), mate is traditionally drunk from a gourd (unhelpfully, also called a *mate*) via a straw called a *bombilla*.

PEPPERMINT

We all know a mug of peppermint tea helps digestion. The ancient Egyptians, one of the most medically advanced ancient cultures, cultivated and used peppermint leaves for indigestion. The ancient Romans and Greeks also took peppermint to soothe dodgy stomachs. The active ingredient in peppermint is menthol, which is an organic compound that produces a cooling sensation when applied to the mouth or skin. Alternative therapies include gargling with peppermint tea three times a day to help soothe a sore throat.

The chemistry of tea

We all know tea as a delicious drink in a cup or in its raw state as a lovely shiny, green leaf. That's really all we need to know, but if you did ever stop to wonder what's actually inside that leaf or what might be in your cup as a result, then the following guide to the "chemistry of tea" may provide a few welcome answers.

Of course, as with any science, when we delve deeper nothing is quite black or white (with the exception of black holes, of course). Tea chemistry is no different. A raw tea leaf may contain many thousands of chemical compounds, which can differ as to where in the world the tea is grown, its altitude, the climate, or maybe the time of year it's harvested or even from where on the bush (top tip or leaf from further down the stem) it's plucked. Those chemicals may then be altered again as that leaf first becomes processed and then again when that processed leaf is infused in hot or boiling water.

An expert tea taster, like Louise, will tell you that it is the art of a tea master who will determine the quality and taste of a tea, as they know exactly when to pluck the leaf, how long to wither and ferment, roll or crush, pack and store and, ultimately, make the tea for optimum pleasure. However, a scientist might be able to explain what's going on during all these stages by referring to the changes in chemical composition of the leaf and the ultimate result on flavor. They are probably both right, but until someone invents a machine that will replace the art and knowledge of a tea master (please don't), we'll go with Louise.

But for wannabe science buffs, here's a guide to what's in a tea leaf:

POLYPHENOLS
It's these natural compounds that give tea its astringency. In green tea the polyphenols are best known as catechins, the "big daddy" of them being epigallocatechin gallate (or EGCG to those, like us, who can't pronounce the full name). It's on these little beauties that much scientific research regarding the antioxidant properties of tea are focused.

AMINO ACIDS
The prevalent amino acid in tea is L-theanine, and tea is one of the few plants that contains this little wonder. Most of the amino acids in tea are changed to polyphenols by the action of the sun. The more sun, the lower the amino acid content, and vice versa. Thus, shade-grown tea used for Matcha has higher concentrations of amino acids than regular tea. Much research is being conducted into whether L-theanine promotes alpha brain wave activity and, with caffeine, induces a state of "mindful alertness" when drinking tea. Maybe it does, maybe it doesn't, but that's how we feel when drinking tea, so who are we to argue?

ALKALOIDS
These usually bitter-tasting compounds occur naturally in plants, with the best known in tea being the infamous caffeine. Some people crave it for its stimulant properties, others avoid it for the same reason. As with many things in life, everything in moderation is probably the best advice.

ENZYMES
Basically enzymes make tea leaves go brown during the fermentation (oxidization) process. If they are prevented from doing their oxidation work, then the leaf stays green. Black tea, green tea; it's the enzymes that make all the difference. We have enzymes in our bodies: they help us digest our food and drinks—they're chemical catalysts for lots of reactions.

PIGMENTS
The world would be a monochromatic place without pigments, because plants wouldn't have any color. These naturally occurring compounds, such as chlorophyll (which gives plants their green color) and beta-carotene (which makes carrots orange) determine what color a plant will be. If a green leaf is allowed to oxidize (during fermentation) the chlorophyll will morph into black pigments known as pheophytins. Other pigments found in tea are carotenes, which are orange and xanthophylls, which are yellow.

CARBOHYDRATES
Including sugars and starches, carbohydrates are the energy stores of plants. When we eat the plants, we break them down to give us energy. In tea, carbohydrates fuel the enzymatic reactions during oxidation.

MINERALS
There are up to 28 minerals found in tea, the most common being fluorine, which has been known to prevent tooth decay. Our bodies need small amounts of many minerals to work properly.

VOLATILES
Without these compounds, food wouldn't have a smell or a taste. They are light and evaporate readily from foods, so are lost over time unless protected. Tea may contain thousands of flavor and aroma compounds, many of which occur during its processing, and will ultimately determine the exact flavor of the tea.

Who knew?

Tea does not contain tannin acid! Tannins is an old-fashioned term for the polyphenols in black tea. The name was coined because it was noted that tea could stain objects a brown color in a manner similar to the way tannic acid tans leather. Nowadays it is often used to describe the mouth-drying effect (astringency) of tea and wine, etc. However, we prefer to call the compounds responsible for this effect by their correct name: polyphenols!

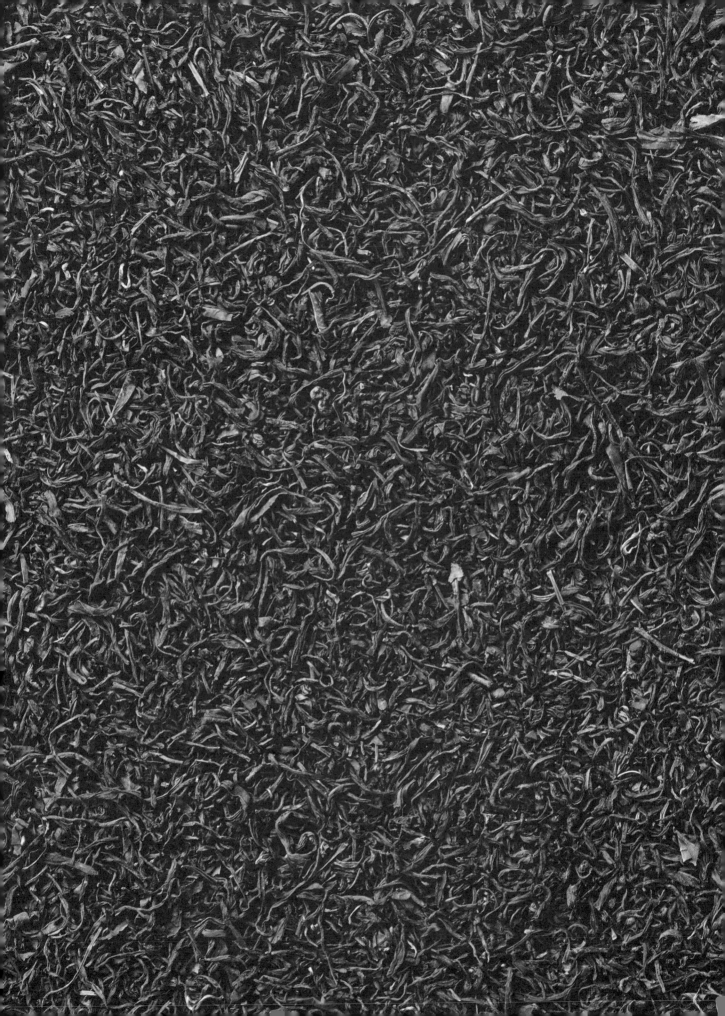

DRINKING TEA

This page Mao Feng green tea.

The job of a tea taster

Fully trained tea tasters are few and far between, so we are superproud to be able to say that teapigs teas have been tasted and selected by an expert with over 15 years' experience. Louise has tasted thousands and thousands of cups of teas over the years. After starting her training at Tetley tea, which involved slurping and spitting at a rate of over 200 to 500 cups per day, she then took off around the world visiting tea estates and buying tea direct from estates or at auctions.

GET TO KNOW THE INDUSTRY

As long as you are not color blind you can develop the skills to become a tea taster. Developing the palate is a bit of an endurance test, tasting hundreds and hundreds of cups of different kinds of teas over and over again. But it's not all slurping and spitting for a tea taster, you're also responsible for buying tea—via auctions, via brokers, or direct from tea estates. Traveling to tea estates is an essential element of the role—understanding the season and the current production while also building relationships is a key part of the job. This can mean traveling to some of the most extreme, remote and beautiful locations around the world—I know it sounds tough, but someone's got to do it!

> **Wouldn't it be dreadful to live in a country where they didn't have tea?**
>
> Noël Coward
> *English playwright, director, actor and singer*

Left Various tea samples spread out on a table during a tasting session.

Opposite Men tasting tea in an English tea-trading house, circa 1932. The tasters stand on one side and their colleagues take down the tasting notes.

EDUCATING YOUR TASTE BUDS

While you can perfect slurping from a spoon in a few weeks, distinguishing flavors and identifying mouthfeel takes a good while longer. As you slurp and swill the tea around your mouth, the layers of taste appear. Head notes are the tastes that are identified immediately; these first impressions of flavor allow you to immediately categorize the tea as good, bad, or great.

The further assessment in the mouth helps to decide whether the tea really makes the grade.

ACCESSORIES FOR THE JOB

There can't be many jobs where the requirements are a big spoon, plenty of North-facing light, and a bucket on wheels. But to be a professional tea taster all these things are essential. The big, flat, soup-style spoon is to get a good slurp. The slurp is needed to lift the tea from the spoon into the mouth along with plenty of oxygen, to get the flavor up into the nostrils for a thorough taste assessment. Lots of North-facing light is ideal for looking at the color and reflection on the meniscus of the tea. The bucket on wheels —called a spittoon—is for spitting out the tea after tasting. No one should literally drink hundreds of cups of tea a day.

Once you have the kit and look the part in an apron (it can get messy), it's time to get started. Large batches of tea are tasted in one go, if you have the space and the help. A tea buyer or tea taster will prepare themselves for an upcoming auction by tasting the auction catalog. Then, they'll be able to narrow down which teas they'll buy (or bid on) at auction.

Opposite Tasting the auction catalog in India. Each tea has a number to be examined easily.

HOW DOES IT TASTE?

You've already heard (left) that slurping is positively encouraged and that there's a special spoon for the job. You might think that anyone can slurp, well they can to a point, but perfecting the action of slurping tea does take some time and practice. Dribbling down the chin in the first few weeks of tea tasting is totally normal and expected, hence the need for the apron!

Using a large soup-style spoon means that you can take in a deep breath at the same time as sucking the liquid into your mouth. A large, loud slurp brings oxygen into your mouth, helping the flavor to circulate. Up to 90% of taste is picked up using your sense of smell. Our tongues, on the other hand, are excellent at detecting the five essential tastes and these give us our initial impression of tea: sweet, salty, acidic, bitter, and umami (a word from Japanese, meaning "a pleasant savory taste").

As well as the taste of the tea, you'll identify the way in which the tea feels in the mouth (known, unsurprisingly, as mouthfeel). What is the weight of the tea? Is it closer to custard rather than water? Does it have an oily character? Is it very drying or astringent? All such elements are all important when it comes to blending teas (see below).

THE NITTY GRITTY: Assessing the look of the tea

First up comes a visual assessment—of both the tea leaves themselves and their brew or liquor. The dry leaf—how does this look? Large or small? Cut or twisted? Stalk, bud, or tip? This leaf assessment gives us an indication of what we are about to taste—almost a sneak preview.

When it comes to assessing the liquor—we look for three aspects: color, brightness, and clarity.

 1 Color—this varies hugely depending on the manufacturing style and the quality of the tea. Even within the same region, there can be a wide variation in color—African teas range from dark, rich, red teas to bright, light, and yellow teas, for instance.

 2 Brightness—this is literally the light reflection from the top of the cup. Brits generally like an amber color brew with a bright appearance.

 3 Clarity—how clear is the brew? If we are looking at green, white, or oolong tea (that is any tea you would drink without milk), clarity is important too—who'd want to drink a cloudy, murky-looking cup of tea? Not me.

BLENDING TEA Many teas are drunk as a blend of more than one type; there are **single-estate teas** but they are in the minority. Professional tea tasters have their own **language** to grade and identify teas (see Tea geek speak, pages 122–123), which allows us to know which standard the teas are and how they can be used in blending.

Tea is incredibly **sensitive** and will easily pick up nearby smells—a bonfire, for example, or, one of my favorites, Brazilian tea with a **hint of coconut**. Some characteristics are not noticeable once the tea is blended, but there is no hiding a burned tea!

Once you have traveled to the estate, learned to slurp, and purchased the tea, the job of a tea taster can then be down to **blending** the tea. The art of blending is all about **developing consistency**. A loyal tea customer who regularly buys a certain brand of tea will be looking for it to **taste the same every time**. But because every batch of tea produced tastes ever so slightly different, a tea taster's work is cut out to adjust the blend so that it always tastes the same. The **grading** helps to simplify the process. When the tea arrives at the point of packing it will be graded again. The final blend will be made up (by hand blend) before actual production to check the blend recipe is "on standard" before committing to packing.

Tasting tea like a pro

A professional tea taster may take anything from five years upward to develop a palate for tasting tea and a vocabulary to be able to describe it, so that they are able to blend teas to make the tastiest cup. Here, our expert Louise gives you tips on tasting tea.

When tasting teas, as well as making the right strength of brew and going through the right motions to extract all the flavors and characters of a tea (see below), we also make sure we taste the teas in the correct order. For example, it is no good tasting peppermint leaves first as the flavor is so strong that it will kill your palate for the rest of the session. Generally, taste pure tea from the tea bush (green tea, white tea, black tea, and oolong tea) first and then move onto the herbals.

IT'S A CASE OF SCRUTINIZE, SNIFF, SLURP, AND SPIT!

SCRUTINIZE: HOW DOES IT LOOK?
Like me, you'll be looking for two things with regard to the appearance of the tea: color and brightness. Use white porcelain vessels (cups and bowls) so that the color sings loud. And when you're looking at brightness, look at the reflection from the top of the meniscus, or the ring at the edge of the cup or bowl.

SLURP: HOW DOES IT TASTE AND FEEL?
As we mentioned before, flavor is actually a combination of smell and taste. So, inhaling and slurping means that you'll get the flavors up into your nose and then the tea will run all around your thousands of taste buds. Will you find a tea that uses any one of my top 5 favorite tea descriptions (opposite)?

Once you've slurped the tea, think about the tea's mouthfeel. When describing how it feels in your mouth, you might want to use words such as "tingly," "drying," "oily," or "creamy."

SNIFF: HOW DOES IT SMELL?
Since smell is intricately intertwined with taste, it's really important to inhale the aromas of the tea. Do this immediately before you slurp.

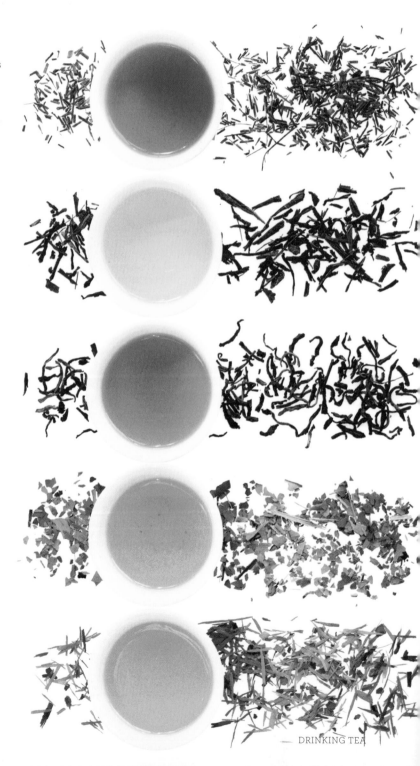

144

THE TEA TASTER'S BREW When tasting tea, follow all the same rules regarding water, temperature, and brew time (see Our unbreakable rules for making a cup of tea, pages 148–149), but with the exception of doubling the quantity of tea. By making tea superstrong, I can make sure that my "superpalate" can detect all the flavors and the quality of each cup or bowl of tea tasted; so give that a try as well when you're tasting.

I traditionally taste tea using white pots and bowls, which give the loose leaves lots of space to infuse fully and the water added is measured exactly. I have to say that there is a bit of an art to pouring the tea from the pot into the bowl without spilling the contents all over the table. I think after my 15 years of tea tasting, I've just about mastered that!

HOW TO SLURP
Use a large, flat soup-style spoon, like I do, to take a spoonful of tea to your mouth. As the loaded spoon arrives, inhale, purse your lips, and take a huge loud slurp. (The louder the slurp the better, as it brings in lots of oxygen, so that the flavors taste livelier.)

SPIT—DON'T SWALLOW
To experience the full flavor of the tea, you'll need to spit it out (rather than swallowing it straightaway, which would mean that lots of the flavor would be lost). Tea tasters use spittoons and trainee tasters have to clean out these rancid buckets on wheels! And we were all trainees once!

MY TOP 5 TEA TASTING TERMS
Every tea taster has a huge vocabulary to be able to express and describe all the flavors of a tea. These are my top 5 favorite expressions, though it has to be said not necessarily my favorite tastes. Goaty tea, anyone?

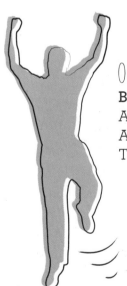

01
BRISK IT'S LIKE A FAST WALK ALL OVER YOUR TONGUE.

03
GOATY WELL, UM, TASTES OF GOAT.

02
TOASTY A LITTLE OVERCOOKED, LIKE DARK BROWN TOAST!

04
FUSTY THINK OF THE SMELL OF A DUSTY OLD CLOSET, AND THAT'S IT!

05
RJ TASTES OF RASPBERRY JAM. DELICIOUS!

The perfect vessel

As we've seen throughout the book, tea is far from a "one size fits all" product. There are so many types of tea and it's drunk across the world in so many different ways and for numerous occasions. Not surprisingly, then, there happens to be a diverse array of vessels for preparation and drinking. One common thing, though, seems to be that just as we each have our favorite way of making tea, we also have a favorite cup, mug, or glass to drink it from.

This page, clockwise from top A glass of hot tea on a saucer; a cast-iron teapot; and a mug of tea..

Opposite, clockwise from top left Cup being filled from a samovar; a glass of mint tea; bone china teacups; a silver Turkish teapot; and gourds with *bombilla* from Argentina for drinking mate; clay cup for chai, India.

OUR UNBREAKABLE RULES FOR MAKING A CUP OF TEA

Now, we want everyone to drink real tea and enjoy drinking real tea. So, here are our basic seven rules for making the perfect cup of tea, every time. Now, repeat after me ... I must only use freshly drawn water, boil it to the right temperature, use top-notch tea with just the right amount of water, brew for 3 minutes, and add milk, as desired. Most importantly, enjoy drinking your tea!

RULE 1

ONLY EVER USE FRESHLY DRAWN WATER

It might be a while since you've drawn any water from a well, if ever, but when we say "freshly drawn water" what we mean is water straight from the faucet. Leaving water in the kettle and boiling it over and over again will make the tea taste "flat." Why fresh each time? Well, then you get a good shot of oxygen in the water and that makes the tea taste oh-so good.

RULE 2

HEAT THE WATER TO THE CORRECT TEMPERATURE

Too hot? Too cold? Aah, just right! If Goldilocks liked tasting tea, she'd surely have something to say about the temperature of the water you use to brew tea. And we do too, and it depends on what tea you're drinking.

Black tea and herbal infusions need boiling water and that means 212°F (100°C).

Green tea, white tea, and oolong don't like boiling water as it will scorch the leaves and take away from their delicate flavor. Technically, you are supposed to use water at 176°F (80°C), but seeing as few of us have a thermometer to hand when making a cup just click your kettle off before it boils or let it cool a little once it has boiled.

RULE 3

ONLY EVER USE QUALITY TEA

This is a biggie (particularly for us). A nice cup comes from brewing nice tea leaves. Don't scrimp when it comes to the quality of the tea. Your taste buds will thank you for it.

RULE 4

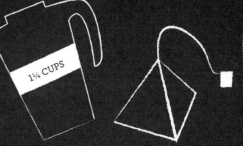

USE JUST THE RIGHT AMOUNT OF WATER

In technical terms, this is the "tea to water ratio"—it's easy to go wrong on this one. Obviously, a gallon of water and one tea leaf won't make a great brew. So, use one whole leaf mesh bag (or tea bag or 1 teaspoon of loose-leaf tea) per person and add enough water for an average sized mug (that's 1¼ cups /300ml).

RULE 5

BREW FOR 3 MINUTES

Quality tea has big leaves (rather than dusty sweepings off the floor!) and so they need a good brew time. Don't dunk and run. It takes time— 3 minutes, on average—for the tea leaves to infuse and release their flavor into the water.

RULE 7

ENJOY THE YUMMY TEA

Let the brew cool—once the tea has been separated from the water it is good to let it cool a little. Not only will piping hot water burn your mouth, but it will also stop you from tasting the yummy tea flavors you have just been brewing.

RULE 6

WARM THE POT

This really does make a difference if you are making black tea. There is simply no point in putting boiling water into a freezing-cold teapot, it just lowers the temperature of the water straightaway—think of it like putting hot food on a cold plate—plus, the taste won't be half as good. Whether or not you want to go and keep your teapot all cozy with a knitted cover is another thing; though, there's no harm in that.

MILK IN FIRST, SECOND, OR NEVER?

1. Black tea and rooibos taste good with milk.
2. Herbals, green tea, white tea, and oolong are best enjoyed without the white stuff (milk).
3. If you are brewing in a pot and are pouring into a cup—put the milk in first then add the brewed tea.
4. If you are brewing in a mug—pour the milk in second after the tea leaves or tea bag has been removed.

WHOLE LEAF, BIG LEAF vs DUSTY TEA BAGS AND SWEEPINGS

One simple way to get a better cup is to go big. I'm not talking mug size here (though I do like a large mug myself) but leaf size. Here I sum up the simple differences between what I call big tea and small tea. As you'll soon discover, ditching the paper tea bag is definitely the way forward.

BIG LEAF

- Looks pretty! Beautiful large orthodox leaf tea and infusions look fabulous.

- Tastes amazing! Quality whole leaf teas have complex flavors—delicate or strong, subtle or powerful.

- Tastes amazing! Ok again, but small batches, packed loose or into those delicate-looking pyramidal mesh bags mean a superfresh and pure-tasting flavor profile.

- Huge variety. Big-leaf, quality artisan teas tend to be seasonal and from a small production batch and offer lots of variety!

- Economical. The same leaves can be steeped multiple times for several cups of tea, saving money as you do so (not advisable for black tea—but for herbals, green, and oolong, go for it!).

SMALL LEAF*

- Ugly duckling! Call us superficial but chopped up tea leaves just don't look as good.

- Big-quantity, small-leaf, low-quality tea will mean a simplistic taste profile and lack-luster appearance.

- Tastes like a tea bag. Tea that's made from a tea bag, tastes like a tea bag, in our opinion. Since tea picks up scents, tea encased in paper can taste of the paper.

- Consistent. Some people like things to always taste the same so tea bag brands have to blend tea to taste consistently the same. However, one of the wonders of tea is that it is seasonal and subject to amazing variation, taste-wise.

- One-off. All the flavor is extracted after just one steeping; it's then thrown away.

*There are some great smaller-leaf teas out there, so this includes some generalizations!

The evolution of the tea temple

We have taken the finest whole-leaf teas and herbal infusions from all over the world, blended them to taste great and then, to make brewing easier and just a bit neater, we have popped them into our very own tea temples.

See-through—nothing is hidden, you can see the beautiful whole leaf.

Portion control—1 teaspoon is a great generic measure; but 1 teaspoon of mint is just not enough and, in my opinion, 1 teaspoon of yerba mate is too much. We have optimised the amount of tea to make the perfect brew every time.

Room to brew—no one likes small spaces. Giving the big leaves a big space allows them to stretch and unfurl and release their big flavors.

Biodegradable—our tea temples are made from corn starch, so they're "green."

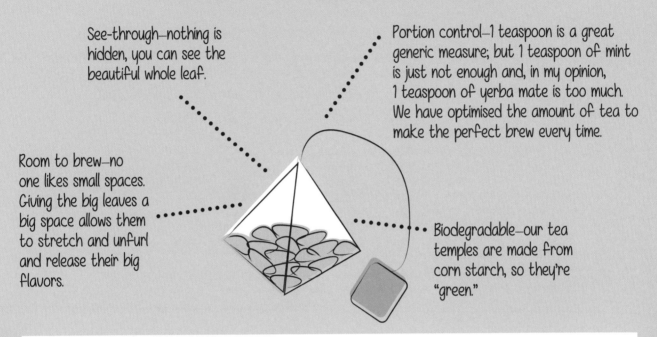

Big leaf

Small leaf

A LITTLE TEA ETIQUETTE

As with any custom or ritual that has been so embedded in history, tea comes with its own set of do's and don'ts. Of course, as tea is drunk the world over, there are some quite specific rules depending upon where you may be.

What <u>not</u> to do

As a general rule, if you'd like to be admired as a true British gentleman or lady when taking your tea, then you'd be best advised never to:

X let your teaspoon crash against the sides of your dainty bone china cup; it's just plain vulgar

X leave your teaspoon in your cup; it must always be placed on the saucer with the handle pointing in the same direction as the cup handle

X cradle your cup with your fingers; hold the handle with your thumb and forefinger but don't ever let your pinky extend out; apparently, it's seen as extravagant and attention seeking

X allow your saucer to travel further than 12 inches (30cm) from your cup

X sip from your spoon (unless, of course, you are a tea taster like Louise)

X swirl your tea around your cup, as you might with wine, for instance

X slurp; absolutely don't slurp, just sip.

Of course, if you just want to enjoy your tea and make it in a nice big mug, then you can do any or all of the above and no one will think any the worse of you! Just be sure to make your brew following our unbreakable rules (see page 148) to get the best out of your tea and enjoy it anytime, anywhere.

Globetrotting tea drinkers: be aware!

Here are a few things to take on board for when you're drinking tea in a foreign country and want to be on your best behavior.

Vietnam
An offer of tea at a reception or meeting is a ritual form of hospitality and should not be refused.

Russia
Don't hesitate to have your tea with a piece of cake, as it is considered quite rude to serve the tea "naked."

India
Reluctantly decline the first offer of tea and let your host insist. Then, after some insistence, politely cave in.

Germany
Don't stir if you've been made an East Frisian tea cloud (see page 30).

Japan
Always taste your tea first before adding sugar or milk.

Argentina
Don't use the *bombilla* (straw) to stir the yerba mate in a gourd.

China
Express your thanks by gently tapping two fingers on the table. Just two, mind.

Morocco
If in a souk, finish your tea before haggling.

Turkey
Since it is offered all the time and everywhere, it is a gesture of hospitality and you must always take the tea, even if you only put it to your lips or just take a few sips.

Egypt
Always accept the cup of tea and/or coffee. Never pour your own drink. Even if you don't want it, accept it anyway, and simply don't drink it. If you refuse, your host may feel rejected.

Confessions of a tea dunker

Do you like to dunk cookies into your tea? I do. If you're not sure what I'm on about, then let me give you a definition of the verb "dunk." *Dunk: to dip food into a drink before eating it.* Sounds straightforward, but in reality it's so much more complex than that. Read on to find out why.

I realize that dunking cookies into tea may be a very British thing to do (although I have heard that Americans dip Oreos into milk and Aussies like to dip a Tim Tam in their brew), but how and where did this ritual originate?

Could it have come from one of the major tea-producing nations, such as China or India? Perhaps it was a Mayan pastime, originally using hot chocolate instead of tea and devised to keep them occupied after their calendar-making came to a halt? Or could it have been the Ancient Romans, who invented pretty much everything else? Despite some thorough research, my dear friends Google and Wikipedia failed to come up with a definite conclusion, at which point I decided to stop searching its origins and instead simply grabbed a cookie and raised a cup to salute the fact that the glorious practice remains with us.

Who knew?

Some research has the roots of dunking cookies aboard naval vessels. The incredibly dry cookies (aimed at keeping the sailors nutrition levels up) kept really well for the long voyages of those times, but they were inedible unless dunked into something repeatedly—whether it was tea or rum is another matter.

SO, WHY DO WE DUNK?

It seems that there is just something inordinately satisfying about eating a warm, wet cookie; the taste and texture of that just-soaked crumb brings with it a heart-warming comfort. Our taste buds work best when we eat warm or hot foods rather than cold, so our taste buds are telling us to dunk into a hot brew.

DARING TO DUNK

How brave are you when it comes to dunking? Are you a single dipper or do you like to double or, even, triple dunk? Of course, the cookie itself matters here but it's also the thrill of running the gauntlet of getting that soggy crumb to your mouth without it ending up down your front. In my mind, it's akin to Russian roulette with cookies. Will you overdo it ever so slightly and lose half of the cookie to your milky brew? It's a risky business—just like deciding to twist rather than stick in a game of Blackjack or to carry on driving when the fuel gauge is flashing and the highway sign says "Next gas station in 1 mile or 67 miles."

Daring to dunk just one more time—and getting away with it—is so rewarding, that I can't help but try it; afterward tell anyone who cares (and plenty of people who don't).

THE BEST DUNKABLE COOKIES

From personal experience, I find the type of cookie is terribly important. Firm-textured, dense and tightly bound cookies, such as Rich Tea and Graham crackers, are good bets; crumbly and brittle chocolate chip cookies, for instance, are just asking for trouble. Some purists would say that a chocolate-coated cookie is cheating—like applying a layer of clear nail varnish to a buckeye (did anyone else do that, or was it just me?)—while others would add that the chocolate meltiness adds an extra pleasurable sensation. I say that, provided the cookie goes with the tea (sweet or neutral rather than salty, and black or rooibos tea, not green or white), you are very much the author of your own dunking destiny.

WHAT WE LIKE TO DUNK

A quick straw poll around the teapigs office revealed the following preferences:

Nick Everyday Brew with milk, Bourbon creams (the cookie, not the booze)
Louise Earl Grey Strong, no milk, Rich Tea cookie
Nikki Darjeeling Earl Grey with milk, ginger cookie
Nicole Everyday Brew, Rich Tea cookie—nice and soggy
Tori Iced licorice & mint, mint cookie—double mint!
Lucy Darjeeling Earl Grey, Graham cracker
Reece Superfruit, pink wafer
Valerie Rooibos, dark-chocolate Graham cracker
Rosie Chai, oat cookie
Rachel Earl Grey Strong, fruit shortcake
Sofia Everyday Brew, chocolate chip cookie
Reggie Rooibos Crème Caramel, chocolate cookie
Juliana Everyday Brew, Bourbon creams cookie

WHAT TEA MOOD ARE YOU IN TODAY?

Tung Ting oolong

ADVENTUROUS

White

Rhubarb & ginger

Licorice & mint

RETRO

Sweet ginger

Darjeeling

Chocolate & mint

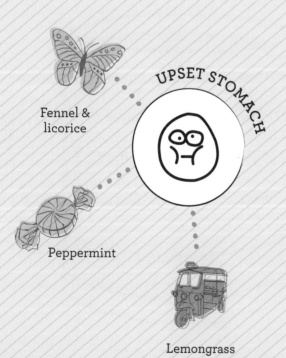

Fennel & licorice

UPSET STOMACH

Mao Feng green

BLOATED

Peppermint

Lemongrass

Matcha

Lemon & ginger

Earl Grey

HUNGOVER

Green tea
with mint

SLEEPY

Chilli chai

Yerba
mate

English
breakfast

Matcha

Chai

Earl Grey
strong

Chocolate

INDULGENT

Chamomile

Rooibos
crème
caramel

STRESSED

Chocolate
& mint

Apple &
cinnamon

GRUMPY

Rooibos

Jasmine

Hibiscus &
mixed berries

Winter-
spiced
rooibos

Genmaicha

RECIPES

This page Rhubarb and ginger tea.

TEA-INFUSED BEEF ON A GREEN PAPAYA SALAD WITH WASABI DRESSING

People have been using tea to flavor meats and fish for many, many years in Asia. Tea is usually mixed with oils and spices to form a marinade, giving the meat or fish a very aromatic and delicate tealike flavor. We love this beef and papaya salad.

SERVES 2

FOR THE TEA-INFUSED BEEF

1 tablespoon yerba mate or Tung Ting oolong whole leaf tea
finely grated zest of 1 orange (use the juice for the salad)
4 tablespoons olive oil
14 ounce (400g) steak (fillet or top round)

FOR THE PAPAYA SALAD WITH WASABI DRESSING

3 garlic cloves
a pinch of salt
3 tablespoons unsalted, roasted peanuts
½ teaspoon wasabi paste
finely grated zest and juice of 1 lime
juice of 1 orange
1 tablespoon fish sauce
1 tablespoon rice vinegar
1 green papaya, about 14 ounces (400g)
1 large carrot
1 cup (100g) bean sprouts
lettuce leaves, such as Boston or Cos, to serve

1 First, prepare the marinade for the beef. Place the tea leaves in a mortar and pestle or a spice grinder and grind to a fine dust, then sift. Add the orange zest and olive oil and stir. Rub this mix into the beef, cover, and let marinate for 1 to 2 hours (in the refrigerator or at room temperature).

2 Preheat the oven to 350°F (180°C).

3 Now, for the salad dressing. Drop the garlic into a mortar and pestle with the salt and bash to crush well. Add 2 tablespoons of the peanuts and continue bashing until you get a coarse paste. Scrape into a large serving bowl and whisk in the wasabi, lime zest, and juice. Then, stir in the orange juice, fish sauce, and rice vinegar.

4 Next, peel the papaya, cut in half lengthwise then place cut side down on a board and slice thinly. Cut again into thin, long matchstick strips and add them to the serving bowl.

5 Peel the carrot, cut in half then slice each piece into thin slices and again into long matchstick strips and tip into the bowl along with the bean sprouts. Now, toss everything together well.

6 To cook the beef, heat an ovenproof pan on high heat and sear the meat all over. Transfer to the preheated oven and cook for 3 to 5 minutes. Remove from the oven, lift the steak onto a plate, and let rest for 10 minutes.

7 Thinly slice the beef and arrange on top of the papaya salad and lettuce leaves, sprinkle with the remaining peanuts, and serve.

CHICKEN TEA BROTH
WITH GREEN TEA SOBA NOODLES AND MARBLED TEA EGGS

In this typical Asian recipe, there's tea in the broth, tea in the noodles, and tea in the eggs—we love that! We think marbled eggs look like something only a kitchen genius could produce, so go ahead and impress your guests with this unusually artistic and very warming broth.

SERVES 4 TO 6

FOR THE CHICKEN
2 tablespoons sesame oil
2-inch (5-cm) piece of fresh ginger root, finely grated
2 garlic cloves, crushed with a pinch of salt
1 tablespoon Shaosing rice wine or sherry
¼ teaspoon freshly ground white pepper
1 tablespoon fish sauce
4 boneless chicken thighs (about 14 ounces/400 g)

FOR THE MARBLED TEA EGGS
6 eggs
6⅓ cups (1.5 liters) water
1 cup (250ml) dark soy sauce
2 star anise
2 tablespoons Tung Ting oolong whole leaf tea
1 cinnamon stick
a pinch of dried red pepper flakes
1 tablespoon Sichuan peppercorns (optional)

FOR THE HERB SALSA
½ cup (25g) minced cilantro leaves
1 cup (25g) mint, minced
1 green chili, minced
2 garlic cloves, minced
1 tablespoon chopped pistachios
3 tablespoons sesame oil
3 tablespoons rice vinegar
finely grated zest of 1 lime
salt and freshly ground black pepper

FOR THE BROTH
6⅓ cups (1.5 liters) water
6 tablespoons green whole leaf tea
a pinch of salt
7 ounces (200g) green tea soba noodles
7 ounces (200g) green leaves (baby spinach or small leaves pak choi), chopped
12 ounces (350g) edamame (soy beans), peas or skinned fava beans, defrosted if frozen
6 scallions, finely sliced
1 tablespoon black sesame seeds
wasabi paste, optional or to serve

1 Mix the sesame oil, ginger, garlic, and Shaosing together and season with white pepper and fish sauce in a bowl. Cut the chicken into bite-size pieces and stir together well. Let marinate for at least an hour or overnight in the refrigerator.

2 Next, prepare the marbled tea eggs. Bring a small pan of water to a boil and gently lower in the eggs. Bring back to a boil and simmer for 5 minutes. Take them out of the water and refresh straightaway with cold water. Then, using the back of a teaspoon, gently tap and crack the eggshell all over, but be careful to keep the shell intact; you're not removing the shell at this stage.

3 Pour the measured water into a pan with all of the remaining ingredients. Bring the mixture to a boil, then immediately turn the heat to low. Simmer gently for 20 minutes, then turn off the heat, add the cracked eggs, cover with a lid, and let the eggs steep for a few hours or overnight. Then, carefully remove the egg shells to reveal the marbled effect beneath.

4 Mix all the ingredients for the salsa together in a small bowl and set aside while you make the broth. Pour the measured water into a large pan, bring to a boil, then remove from the heat and stir in the tea leaves. Cover and let steep for 10 minutes, then strain through a fine strainer into a clean pan.

5 Bring the pan back to a boil with a pinch of salt, stir in the soba noodles, return to a boil again, then pour in 1 cup (240ml) of cold water. Repeat this method twice more, then the noodles should be just tender. Hook out the noodles with tongs and set aside. Add the chicken pieces to the broth, along with any marinade and simmer gently for 5 to 10 minutes or until tender.

6 Taste for seasoning and adjust to taste, stir in the green leaves, edamame, scallions, and tea eggs—keep the eggs whole as they look so beautiful—and simmer for a few minutes more or until the leaves are just tender. Serve sprinkled with the sesame seeds, some wasabi, if you like, and a spoonful of salsa.

TEA-SMOKED DUCK BREASTS WITH SPICED PEARS

This recipe—from Lindy Wildsmith's amazing book *Cured*—can be made with commercially smoked duck breast, but if you'd like to have a go at hot smoking your own then this tea-smoked duck is even more delicious. It is so simple and the duck is so unbelievably tender. It's best served warm.

SERVES 4 AS AN APPETIZER

4¼ ounces (125g) arugula, spinach, watercress, and beet leaf salad
3½ ounces (100g) green beans, lightly cooked in salted boiling water, drained, plunged into ice water, and drained again
4 scallions, shredded
4-inch (10-cm) piece of cucumber, cut into matchsticks
1¾ ounces (50g) purple radish sprouts (or radishes work well too, sliced thinly)
2 x 5½-ounce (1500g) duck breasts, tea-smoked (see box below)
½ cup (50g) walnut pieces

FOR THE SPICED PEARS

1 cup (250ml) perry vinegar or cider vinegar
¾ ounce (20g) fresh ginger root, peeled
1 garlic clove
½ teaspoon cumin seeds
1 bay leaf
1 star anise
a pinch of ground mace
a pinch of sea salt
½ cup (100g) packed light brown sugar
1 pound 11¾ ounces (750g) firm pears, peeled and cut in half

FOR THE DRESSING

1 teaspoon thyme leaves
2 tablespoons walnut oil
2 tablespoons olive oil
5 teaspoons red wine vinegar
1 teaspoon honey
a pinch of sea salt

1 First, make the spiced pears. Put the vinegar, ginger, garlic, cumin seeds, bay leaf, star anise, mace, salt, and sugar in a pan and bring to simmering point. Cook gently until the sugar has dissolved, then increase the heat and boil for 5 minutes to reduce.

2 Poach the pear halves in the spiced syrup until tender. Set aside 2 pear halves and slice them for this recipe and transfer the rest to a sterilized jar and seal.

3 Next, make the salad dressing. Put all the dressing ingredients in a screw-top jar, replace the lid, and shake well. Taste and adjust as necessary.

4 Smoke the duck breasts, see box below. If you prefer crispy duck skin then sear the duck breast in a hot frying pan or skillet after the smoking and before slicing. Otherwise, slice the tea-smoked duck breasts thinly.

5 Now, to assemble the salad. Put the salad greens, beans, scallion, cucumber, and purple radish sprouts in a bowl. Drizzle over the dressing and toss lightly. Either divide the salad between 4 plates and arrange the pears and the duck breast on the side, sprinkled with the walnut pieces or arrange the duck and pears on top of the salad and serve from the salad bowl—whichever you prefer.

DIY HOT SMOKING WITH TEA You can hot smoke at home without going to the trouble or expense of buying a special kit. Simply use a heavy-based lidded wok or steamer with a cooking rack inside, or use the steamer basket. You can even use a covered heavy-bottom roasting pan with a trivet. If you don't want to ruin said pots and pans forever, line the bottom and sides with several layers of foil. Spread some rice over the bottom of the pan along with some of your favorite tea leaves (a teaspoon or so) to aromatize the duck and sprinkle over some plain sugar, which will be the fuel. Then, place the duck breasts on the rack. Set your improvised smoker over high heat for 10 minutes, which is long enough to ignite the fuel. Unless you have a professional venting system in your kitchen, use a gas barbecue outdoors to ignite your fuel, then it can puff away. Hot smoking is basically cooking with the added element of smoke and therefore you can mostly follow the cooking times you would use for other quick-cooking processes. Duck breasts take 20 to 30 minutes; but, for example, scallops, oysters, mussels, and shrimp would take mere minutes, thin fillets of fish not much longer, with big pieces of meat taking much longer. But there is no substitute for experimenting to achieve the right results. As a general guideline, when the meat or fish turns opaque, it is ready. Happy (tea) smoking!

MAO FENG CILANTRO SHRIMP

Throughout Asia, tea is used in lots of fish dishes. It's popular to smoke fish with tea, but you can use it to add depth to sauces and—in this instance—batters. In this yummy shrimp dish, the batter is light and fragrant and the herb sauce is supertasty.

SERVES 4 AS AN APPETIZER

10½ ounces (300g) shelled raw tiger shrimp, with tail on and deveined

FOR THE HERB SAUCE
⅔ cup (150ml) water
1 tablespoon Mao Feng green whole leaf tea
2 garlic cloves, peeled and sliced
a 2-inch (5-cm) piece of fresh ginger root, finely grated
1 medium red or green chili, seeded and coarsely chopped
3 scallions, chopped
½ cup (25g) chopped cilantro leaves and stalks
1¾ ounces (50g) watercress, chopped
1 small avocado, pitted and peeled
juice of 1 lime
sea salt flakes and freshly ground black pepper

FOR THE BATTER
3 eggs and 3 egg whites
⅔ cup (100g) potato flour
2 tablespoons Mao Feng green whole leaf tea
a small handful of whole cilantro leaves
peanut oil, for deep-frying
lime wedges, to serve

1 To make the sauce, in a pan bring the measured water to a boil and add the tea leaves, followed by the garlic, ginger, chili, and scallions. Remove from the heat and let all infuse for 5 minutes.

2 Stir in the chopped cilantro and watercress and stir until wilted. Cool slightly then transfer to a food processor and whiz along with the avocado, lime juice, and a pinch of salt, until smooth. Season with black pepper.

3 Next, get on with the batter. Beat the whole eggs and potato flour in a bowl until smooth. In a separate bowl, whisk the egg whites until they reach soft peaks. Beat one-third of the whites into the flour, along with the tea leaves and cilantro leaves and then gently fold in the rest of the beaten egg whites.

4 Put a wok or deep pan over high heat and fill to a quarter of its depth with peanut oil. Heat the oil to 350°F (180°C), or until a cube of bread turns brown in 15 seconds. Dip the shrimp in the batter one by one and carefully lower them into the oil; you'll need to cook them in several batches. Cook until golden, turning occasionally, then lift from the oil and drain on paper towels. Sprinkle with sea salt and serve hot with lime wedges.

LEMONGRASS TEA-SMOKED MACKEREL WITH RHUBARB RELISH

We think smoked mackerel is delicious. And tea-smoked mackerel, as here, is even more delicous. The relish—made with lemongrass tea and rhubarb—gives you a wonderfully citrus sharpness that works perfectly with the smoky, oily fish.

SERVES 4

FOR THE RHUBARB RELISH

1 cup (200g) superfine sugar
scant ½ cup (100ml) red wine or
    cider vinegar
6 tablespoons lemongrass
    whole leaf tea, tied in a
    cheesecloth bag
1 red chili, minced
6 scallions, finely sliced
1 pound 3½ ounces (550g)
    rhubarb, untrimmed weight
    (1 pound/450g trimmed)

FOR THE MACKEREL

½ cup (100g) light brown sugar
½ cup (100g) rice
3½ ounces (100g) Mao Feng green
    whole leaf tea
4 mackerel fillets, about 5½ ounces
    (150g) each with skin on
salt and freshly ground black
    pepper
oil, for greasing
lime wedges and salad
    greens, to serve

1 First, make the rhubarb relish. In a pan, pop the sugar, vinegar, and tea in the cheesecloth. Bring the liquid to a boil, stirring every now and then to dissolve the sugar. Add the chili, reduce the heat, and simmer for 10 minutes. Add the scallion and cook for another 5 minutes. Finally, add the rhubarb and cook for 3 to 4 minutes or until just tender. Remove from the heat and let cool and infuse. Then squeeze out all the liquid from the cheesecloth bag.

2 Mix the sugar, rice, and tea leaves together and place on a double sheet of foil in the bottom of a large wok and place a trivet on top (you can use a round cake wire tray as the trivet).

3 Season the mackerel and lay each fillet on a piece of parchment paper, skin side up in a single layer on the trivet. Start to heat over moderate heat until the tea just starts to smoulder, then cover very tightly with a lid or a tent of foil. Turn off the heat and let the mackerel cook for 15 minutes.

4 Serve the mackerel with the rhubarb relish, lime wedges, and salad.

MATCHA, CHOCOLATE, AND GINGER TIRAMISU

Why use coffee when you could use tea?! Especially when you could use chocolate tea and Matcha. In this delicious twist on the traditional tiramisu, the tea flavors work great with the creamy mascarpone, and the ginger gives an extra yummy kick.

SERVES 6 TO 8

⅔ cup (150ml) water
4 chocolate flake tea temples
   (or other chocolate whole leaf
   mesh tea bags)
9 ounces (250g) plain sponge,
   chocolate cake or Green Tea
   Pound Cake (see page 173)
2 eggs, separated
3 tablespoons superfine sugar
½ teaspoon vanilla extract
2¼ cups (500g) mascarpone
1 small piece preserved ginger, finely
   chopped (optional)

FOR DECORATION
unsweetened cocoa
Matcha

1 Pour the measured water into a small pan and bring to a boil. Add in the chocolate tea temples (or whole leaf mesh tea bags, if using), then remove the pan from the heat and let infuse for 15 minutes, then squeeze out the tea temples and transfer the liquid into a shallow dish.

2 Cut the cake into 3¼ x ¾-inch (8 x 2-cm) long fingers. Dip each finger into the tea mixture, then use these to line a dish, evenly pouring over any remaining tea.

3 In a bowl, beat the egg yolks with the sugar and vanilla until light, then beat in a little of the mascarpone and then beat in the rest with the chopped preserved ginger.

4 In a separate bowl, whisk the egg whites until they reach soft peaks. Beat one-third of the whites into the mascarpone mixture and then gently fold in the rest. Spoon this mixture over the soaked cake in the dish.

5 Dust with cocoa, sprinkle with a little Matcha powder, cover, and set aside in the refrigerator for at least an hour before serving.

EARL GREY HEARTS

If you love Earl Grey tea then what could be better than Earl Grey-flavored cookies to go with it? This recipe is from *Country Living's* Food & Drink Editor, Alison Walker's book *Handmade Gifts from the Kitchen*—make them for yourself as a treat or give them as a gift for any tea lover.

MAKES 25 TO 30

1¼ cups (175g) all-purpose flour

scant ½ cup (50g) confectioners'
    sugar

1 teaspoon Earl Grey strong whole
    leaf tea

7 tablespoons (100g) butter, softened,
    plus extra for greasing

1 medium egg yolk

1 Put the flour, confectioners' sugar, and tea into a food processor. Add the rest of the ingredients and mix to form a soft dough. Shape into a disk, wrap in plastic wrap, and chill for 20 minutes.

2 Meanwhile, preheat the oven to 375°F (190°C), and lightly grease 2 or 3 baking sheets.

3 Remove the dough from the refrigerator and lightly flour a counter. Roll out to a ¼ inch (5mm) thickness, cut out shapes with a 2-inch (5-cm) heart-shaped cutter (or various sizes) and space apart on the baking sheets.

4 Bake in the preheated oven for 8 to 10 minutes until lightly golden. Let cool on the sheets for a couple of minutes before transferring to wire racks to cool completely. These cookies keep for up to 4 weeks in an airtight container or sealed package.

EARL GREY MACARONS WITH LEMON OR LAVENDER

Macarons are such a treat. Light and delicate, sweet and creamy, and fancy-looking all at the same time. The bergamot flavoring in Earl Grey is just perfect with the almondy loveliness of these macarons. You friends will be impressed too!

MAKES ABOUT 20

FOR THE MACARONS
1½ cups (175g) confectioners' sugar
1⅓ cups (125g) ground almonds
2 tablespoons Earl Grey strong whole
    leaf tea
3 large egg whites
a pinch of salt
¼ cup plus 2 tablespoons (75g)
    superfine sugar

FOR A LAVENDER FILLING
½ tablespoon dried lavender, ground
⅔ cup (75g) confectioners' sugar
7 tablespoons (100g) butter, softened

FOR A LEMON FILLING
7 tablespoons (100g) butter, softened
finely grated zest and juice of
    ½ lemon, plus more juice, to taste
⅔ cup (75g) confectioners' sugar

1 Preheat the oven to 310°F (160°C).

2 Make the macarons. Mix the confectioners' sugar, almonds, and tea leaves in a food processor until they are very finely ground.

3 Whisk the egg whites with a pinch of salt until they form soft peaks, then gradually whisk in the superfine sugar, a spoonful at a time, until the meringue is thick and glossy.

4 Next, fold half of the almond and tea mixture into the meringue and mix well, then fold in the remaining mix, until it is smooth and shiny and has a ribbonlike consistency. Spoon half of the mixture into a pastry bag with a ½-inch (1-cm) tip.

5 Line 2 baking sheets with parchment paper and pipe into 40 small rounds, about 1¼ inches (3cm) across; they will expand just a little when they cook. Let stand at room temperature for 10 to 15 minutes to form a slight skin—you should be able to touch them lightly without any mixture sticking to your finger. Bake for 15 minutes, then remove from the oven, slide the sheets onto wire racks and let cool completely on the paper. Meanwhile, get on with making your choice of fillings.

6 For the lavender filling, mix the dried lavender flowers with the confectioners' sugar in a food processor until very fine then sift into a bowl. In another bowl, beat the butter until light and fluffy then beat in the lavender-flavored confectioners' sugar. It's now ready to use.

7 For the lemon filling, beat the butter with the lemon zest until light and fluffy, then gradually beat in the confectioners' sugar and half of the juice. Once smooth, taste, adding more lemon juice if needed.

8 Sandwich 2 macarons with a teaspoon of your chosen filling and continue in this way to use all the filling and all the macarons to create a batch of these little treats.

CHAI HOT CROSS BUN BREAD AND BUTTER PUDDING

Bread and butter pudding is one of the most comforting desserts. This version uses hot cross buns (genius!) and the chai tea with all its spices adds heaps more warmth and flavor. We love to make them in individual cups for cuteness.

SERVES 6

1¼ cups (300ml) milk
1¼ cups (300ml) light cream
2 tablespoons chai whole leaf tea
2 eggs
¼ cup plus 2 tablespoons (75g) superfine sugar
6 hot cross buns
3½ tablespoons butter, softened

1 Pour the milk and cream into a pan and sprinkle in the chai. Bring to just below a boil, remove from the heat, and then let steep for 5 minutes.

2 Meanwhile, whisk the eggs with the sugar in a bowl and strain the tea-infused cream mixture through a strainer (to remove the tea leaves) and onto the eggs and sugar, whisking all the time. You now have a custard; it will thicken up as it bakes.

3 Cut each hot cross bun horizontally into 3 equally sized slices and butter 1 side of each piece. Place the bottom third of each bun into the bases of six 7-ounce (200-ml) ramekins, mugs, or even large tea cups.

4 Pour a little of the custard into each ramekin or cup, then add the middle section of the buns. Add more of the custard to each until it is all used up, then top with the last slices of the buns, with the cross uppermost. Press slightly but don't submerge the tops. Set aside for 30 minutes to soak. Meanwhile, preheat the oven to 350°F (180°C).

5 Arrange the ramekins or cups in a roasting pan, place in the oven, and carefully fill the pan with boiling water until it comes halfway up the cups. Bake for about 20 minutes or until just cooked, but a bit wobbly in the center. Serve warm but not hot.

GREEN TEA POUND CAKE

Roger Pizey knows a thing or two about cakes and we love his version of this delicious cake (taken from his book *World's Best Cakes*), which uses one of our favorite ingredients—Matcha. In this "East meets West" cake, the subtle flavor of the Japanese green tea infuses a Western pound cake—with fabulous and colorful results.

SERVES 10

2⅔ cups (375g) all-purpose flour
1 teaspoon baking powder
2 tablespoons Matcha
1¼ cups (275g)) butter, softened
1¼ cups plus 2 tablespoons (275g)
    superfine sugar
4 eggs, beaten

1 Preheat the oven to 325°F (170°C), and grease and line a 10-inch long x 3¼ x 3¼-inch (25 x 8 x 8-cm) deep loaf pan with parchment paper.

2 Sift the flour, baking powder, and Matcha together into a bowl.

3 Cream the butter and sugar together until light and fluffy, and then slowly add the eggs, mixing in a little flour halfway through.

4 Add the rest of the flour mixture and mix together until fully combined.

5 Turn the batter into the prepared pan and bake in the preheated oven for 40 to 50 minutes. Let cool for 10 minutes in the pan and then turn out onto a wire rack, then strip off the parchment paper.

6 Serve with green tea or any other delicately flavored tea.

TEA LOAF

Many nations have their own version of this delicious tea loaf, but here's a great tried-and-tested recipe from all-round creative Jane Brocket. This cake has a lovely texture and taste, slices beautifully and is delicious spread with butter and served with hot tea. You can use a basic black tea to soak the fruit or mix it up with aromatic varieties, such as Earl Grey or lapsang souchong.

SERVES 8 TO 10

13 ounces (375g) mixed dried fruit and peel
1 cup (250ml) strained, cold tea (strong, no milk or sugar)
butter, for greasing
¾ cup (150g) packed soft brown sugar
1 egg, lightly beaten
1¾ cups (250g) all-purpose flour
1 heaping teaspoon baking powder
a pinch of mixed spice, grated nutmeg, or ground cloves (optional)
finely grated zest of 1 lemon

1 Begin the night before with soaking the fruit. Put the dried fruit and cold tea in a mixing bowl. Cover and let soak overnight at room temperature.

2 Next day, when you are ready to bake, preheat the oven to 310°F (160°C), and grease and line a 8½ x 4¼ x 2¾-inch (22 x 11 x 7-cm) loaf pan.

3 Add the sugar and egg to the soaked fruit and mix well with a wooden spoon or flexible spatula. Sift in the flour, baking powder, and spice (if using), and mix well until thoroughly combined.

4 Spoon the batter into the prepared loaf pan and level the surface with the back of the spoon. Bake in the center of the oven for 1 to 1¼ hours until a metal skewer or sharp knife inserted into the center of the cake comes out clean.

5 Remove from the oven, transfer to a wire rack, and let cool before turning out of the pan. Serve in slices with or without butter, whichever you prefer.

FRUIT CAKES FROM AROUND THE WORLD We like to maximize the fruitiness of this fruit cake by soaking the dried fruit in a strong brew, just as in Jane Brocket's recipe above. The Welsh fruit loaf—*bara brith*—also uses tea in this way; as does the Irish *barmbrack*, which is brought out at Halloween—this cake has added coins (for good luck). North of the border, the Scots like to use a tot of sherry (rather than tea) in their classic Dundee cake. Elsewhere in the world, other flavors can make yet more delicious fruit cakes. In the Caribbean, for instance, rum is a favorite added flavor; but you'll also find rum in the classic Eastern European fruity cakes, such as Cozonac, which is traditionally eaten at Easter. In the past, American fruit cakes used brandy or a strong alcoholic liqueur but mostly these are alcohol-free nowadays. We reckon they should try our tea-based version!

CHAI AND CHESTNUT MUFFINS
WITH CHILLI CHAI TEA GLAZE

Chestnuts—all comforting and Christmassy—taste amazing in this muffin recipe that uses chai tea (with its warming spices) and a yummy, sticky, chai tea glaze. They are perfect with a steaming mug of chai latte when it's cold outside.

SERVES 6

FOR THE CHAI GLAZE
*scant ½ cup (50g) confectioners'
    sugar*
juice of 1 lemon
*2 chili chai tea temples (or
    4 teaspoons chili chai or chai
    whole leaf tea)*

FOR THE MUFFINS
1 cup (250ml) milk
9 ounces (250g) cooked chestnuts
1 tablespoon chai whole leaf tea
2 eggs, beaten
½ cup (100g) superfine sugar
1¼ cups (180g) all-purpose flour
2 tsp baking powder
a pinch of salt

1 First, make the glaze. Place the confectioners' sugar, lemon juice, and tea temples (or whole leaf tea, if using) into a small pan and heat gently, remove from the heat then set aside to cool and infuse. Meanwhile, pour milk into another pan and pop in the chestnuts and other whole leaf tea. Bring to just below a boil, then remove from the heat and let infuse for 30 minutes.

2 Preheat the oven at 400°F (200°C) and line a 12-hole muffin pan with liners. Meanwhile, beat the eggs in a large bowl and then strain the infused milk over the eggs and beat together. Reserve one-third of the chestnuts from the strainer and transfer the rest to the bowl of a food processor along with the sugar and whiz until smooth. Whisk this into the egg and milk mixture.

3 Next, sift the flour, baking powder, and salt together into a bowl, crumble in the reserved chestnuts, and fold this into the egg mixture.

4 Place a spoonful of batter into each paper liner, filling each just over halfway. Bake for 15 to 20 minutes in a preheated oven, or until golden brown.

5 Remove the pan from the oven and transfer to a wire rack to cool. Lift or strain the tea temples (or tea leaves, if using) from the syrup, and brush it on the top of each muffin while they are still hot (this makes for a shinier glaze) and let cool for 5 minutes before lifting the muffins out of the pan and onto the rack to cool completely.

APPLE AND CINNAMON TEA FLAPJACK

Good-quality fruit and herbal teas made with whole ingredients give you lots of intense flavor. The apple and cinnamon tea make these flapjacks fruity, moist, and generally ultrayummy.

MAKES 24 PIECES

⅔ cup (150ml) boiling water
9 apple and cinnamon tea temples (or 18 teaspoons apple and cinnamon whole leaf tea)
1¼ cups (300g) unsalted butter
¼ cup plus 2 tablespoons (75g) packed light brown sugar
⅓ cup (125g) light corn syrup
1 apple, peeled and grated
2⅓ cups (200g) rolled oats
2⅓ cups (200g) jumbo oats
7 ounces (200g) mixture of seeds and nuts (we used sunflower seeds, pumpkin seeds, goji berries, dried blueberries, dried cranberries, and pine nuts)
a pinch of sea salt

1 Pour the boiling water into a bowl with the tea temples (or whole leaf tea, if using) and let infuse for 1 hour.

2 Preheat the oven to 325°F (170°C), and line a 10 x 12-inch (25 x 30-cm) cookie sheet with parchment paper.

3 Place the butter in a heavy pan over low heat. When the butter has melted, give it a stir, remove from the heat and stir in the sugar and light corn syrup followed by the strained, infused tea (squeeze out the tea temples to get every ounce of flavor out). Stir until well combined, then add the grated apple, oats, the seed and nut mixture, and salt and mix well.

4 Tip the mixture into the prepared cookie sheet and spread evenly, pressing down with the back of a spoon. Bake for 20 to 30 minutes, or until golden.

5 Remove from the oven and let the flapjack cool for a few minutes in the cookie sheet. While it is still warm, mark it into squares with a knife. Once it's completely cold, simply break the flapjack into pieces; they should snap away cleanly where you've marked them. Enjoy with a cup of tea!

JEWISH HONEY CAKE

Traditionally this cake is served at Jewish New Year—Rosh Hashanah—a time to reflect on the past and look forward to the future. We love that tea is involved in such celebrations. The tea makes this cake beautifully moist. This cake works best when it is made a few days before being served, so says chef pâtissier Roger Pizey, as the sweet honey flavors develop over time.

SERVES 8

¾ cup (150g) packed brown sugar
1 egg
1¼ cups (280ml) cold tea (we used
  2 morning glory tea temples or
  4 teaspoons English Breakfast
  whole leaf tea to make a nice brew)
⅔ cup (150ml) vegetable oil
generous ¾ cup (180g) honey
2⅓ cups (330g) self-rising flour
½ teaspoon mixed spice
½ teaspoon ground ginger
½ teaspoon ground cinnamon
1 teaspoon baking soda

1 Preheat the oven to 310°F (160°C), and grease and line an 8-inch (21-cm) round cake pan with parchment paper.

2 Combine the sugar, egg, tea, oil, and honey well in one bowl. In a separate bowl, sift the dry ingredients and then mix everything together.

3 Pour the cake batter into the prepared cake pan and bake for 1 hour or until a toothpick inserted into the center comes out clean.

4 Remove from the oven, let cool for 10 minutes in the pan, and then turn out onto a wire rack and strip off the parchment paper. Enjoy this cake at teatime or after dinner as a tasty dessert.

MATCHA & PISTACHIO CUPCAKES WITH WHITE CHOCOLATE FROSTING

We love anything that contains Matcha (we're total tea nuts after all), but Matcha tastes especially delicious with white chocolate and anything nutty, so these cupcakes are mindblowingly good. Creamy, sweet with a delicate green tea flavor. Yes please!

MAKES 24

1¼ cups (180g) self-rising flour
1 teaspoon baking powder
1 tablespoon Matcha
a pinch of sea salt
generous ¾ cup (180g) unsalted
    butter, softened
scant 1 cup (180g) superfine sugar
½ teaspoon vanilla extract
3 large eggs
⅔ cup (100g) chopped pistachios

FOR THE WHITE CHOCOLATE FROSTING

1¼ cups (300ml) heavy cream
½ vanilla bean
3½ ounces (100g) white chocolate,
    chopped

1 Make the chocolate frosting. Put half of the cream in a pan. Cut the vanilla bean in half lengthwise and scrape out the seeds into the cream, and drop in the bean. Bring to just below a boil then remove from the heat, remove and discard the used bean, and whisk in the chopped chocolate until smooth. Cool then place in the refrigerator and let chill for about an hour.

2 When the frosting's almost ready, preheat the oven to 350°F (180°C), and line 2 12-hole cupcake pans with 24 paper liners.

3 In a bowl, sift the flour, baking powder, Matcha, and salt together.

4 In a separate bowl, beat the butter, sugar, and vanilla together until very smooth. Add the eggs one at a time, adding some flour halfway through, if necessary, and beating well after each addition.

5 Fold the flour mixture into the egg mixture along with three-quarters of the chopped pistachios (keep the rest for decorating later on).

6 Spoon the cupcake batter into the liners and bake for 15 to 20 minutes or until risen and slightly golden.

7 Remove the cupcakes from the oven and transfer to a wire rack to cool for 5 minutes, then remove from the pans and let cool completely.

8 In another bowl, whip the remaining cream until it reaches soft peaks. Beat in one-third of the whipped cream into the chilled chocolate cream mixture and then fold in the remainder. Transfer to a pastry bag ready for decorating the cupcakes. Pipe the frosting onto the cupcakes, spread a little with a knife, and then top with a sprinkle of the remaining chopped pistachios.

MATCHA TRUFFLES

Matcha works so well with chocolate. You can buy these truffles from premium food halls, but it's more fun to make your own, especially when the truffley part is that wondrously bright green.

**MAKES ABOUT
40 TRUFFLES**

FOR THE TRUFFLES
½ cup (120ml) heavy cream
10½ ounces (300g) white
 chocolate, finely chopped
2 tablespoons Matcha,
 plus extra for dusting

FOR THE COATING
3½ ounces (100g) each of white,
 milk, and semisweet chocolate
confectioners' sugar, for dusting

1 Bring the cream to a boil in a small pan. Remove from the heat and tip in the white chocolate and whisk quickly until the chocolate is melted and smooth.

2 Sift in the Matcha and beat well again. Pour the chocolate mixture into a bowl, cover, and chill for 4 to 5 hours or until completely set.

3 Using a teaspoon, scoop out small spoonfuls of the truffle mixture onto a tray or a plate and return to the refrigerator for 10 to 15 minutes.

4 When the mixture has firmed up again, dust the palm of your hand lightly with a little confectioners' sugar and roll each piece of truffle mixture into a neat ball and place back on the tray. Return to the refrigerator while you melt the chocolate.

5 Melt the chocolate in three separate bowls. Using one bowl of melted chocolate at a time, spoon a little of the chocolate onto a plate and roll a ball of truffle evenly around to coat and return to the tray. Repeat with one-quarter of the truffles and place these back in the refrigerator. Repeat with the remaining truffles and melted chocolate, then recoat the first truffles. You'll need to roll the truffles in the melted chocolate about three times, until you've used all the chocolate up and to get a good coating. Roll the remaining quarter of truffles in unsweetened cocoa. Finally, sprinkle all the truffles with a little more Matcha powder before the chocolate sets.

MATCHA AND CHOCOLATE SHORTBREAD

It's hard to imagine a more perfect partner for a cup of tea as William Curley's melt-in-the-mouth recipe marries two of our favorite things—shortbread and Matcha.

MAKES ABOUT 60

1⅓ cups (185g) all-purpose flour, sifted
½ cup (125g) unsalted butter, cut into cubes, at room temperature
scant ⅓ cup (60g) superfine sugar
1 teaspoon Matcha, plus extra for dusting
1 pound 2 ounces (500g) semisweet chocolate, melted, to coat

1 Put all the ingredients, except the chocolate, into a bowl and mix until the ingredients come together in a dough.

2 Remove from the bowl. Roll the dough to ¼ inch (5mm) thick on a lightly floured counter. Cut into 1½-inch (4-cm) squares and transfer to a cookie sheet lined with a nonstick baking mat or parchment paper. Let rest for at least 1 hour in the refrigerator.

3 Preheat the oven to 325°F (160°C). Bake the shortbread in the preheated oven for 20 to 25 minutes until lightly golden. Remove from the oven and transfer to a wire rack to cool. Dip in melted semisweet chocolate and dust with Matcha powder. (If you prefer and have time, you could temper the chocolate so that you keep its wonderful shine.)

LICORICE AND MINT CHOC CHIP ICE CREAM WITH DARK CHOCOLATE TUILLE

Wow, wow, wow! This is 100% our favorite ice cream flavor. Naturally sweet licorice, superfresh mint, semisweet chocolate, and wonderfully creamy ice cream—it's an explosion of amazing flavors. And you can make a chocolate tuille to go with it, if you're feeling fancy.

MAKES 1.4 QUARTS (1.6 LITERS)

FOR THE ICE CREAM

4 cups (1 liter)) whole milk
1¼ cups (300ml) heavy cream
7 tablespoons licorice and mint
    whole leaf tea
6 egg yolks
1¼ cups (250g) sugar
3½ ounces (100g) semisweet
    chocolate, finely chopped, or
    semisweet chocolate chips

FOR THE CHOCOLATE TUILLE
(MAKES ABOUT 20 TUILLES)

⅓ cup (50g) all-purpose flour
1 tablespoon unsweetened cocoa
3½ tablespoons (50g) unsalted butter,
    softened
scant ½ cup (50g) confectioners'
    sugar
1 large egg white, lightly beaten with
    a tiny pinch of salt

1 Pour the milk and cream into a pan and sprinkle in the tea leaves. Bring to a boil, remove from the heat, and steep for 1 hour.

2 Next, whisk the egg yolks with the sugar in a bowl and strain the tea-infused cream mixture through a strainer (to remove the tea leaves) and onto the eggs and sugar, whisking all the time. Pour back into the pan and heat gently, stirring all the time, for about 5 minutes; the mixture will only thicken very slightly. Remove from the heat, pour into a clean bowl, cover with plastic wrap gently pressing it onto the surface of the custard to prevent a skin from forming, then cool and chill completely.

3 Churn the chilled custard in an ice-cream maker. Once ready, stir the chocolate evenly through the ice cream. If you don't have an ice-cream maker, then you can freeze the custard in a plastic container, whisking well every half an hour or so, until evenly slushy, then whiz up in a food processor. Return to the freezer and freeze for another 30 minutes then whiz again until smooth. Stir in the chopped chocolate or choc chips, then freeze until set.

4 While the ice cream is freezing, make the chocolate tuilles. Line a cookie sheet with parchment paper. Sift the flour with the cocoa into a bowl. In a separate bowl, beat the softened butter and confectioners' sugar together until well blended.

5 Gradually beat the egg white into the butter and sugar mixture, then beat in the flour and cocoa a little at a time until you have a smooth mixture. Let rest for 30 minutes.

6 Preheat the oven to 350°F (180°C). Place a teaspoonful of the mixture onto the prepared sheet and, using the back of the teaspoon, working in circular movements, spread the mix out thinly to an even circle about 3 inches (8cm) in diameter. Repeat two or three times, evenly spaced out. Only bake a few at a time as they harden very quickly once out of the oven.

7 Bake for about 5 to 6 minutes or until just set. Remove from the oven quickly and carefully. While the tuilles are still hot, roll quickly around the handle of a wooden spoon, drape over a rolling pin or leave until set. If the tuilles cool and harden before you have the chance to mold them, return the sheet to the oven for a minute or so to soften then mold as above.

8 When ready to serve, remove the ice cream from the freezer to soften (about 10 minutes ahead of serving) then scoop into glasses and serve with the chocolate tuilles.

ICED TEA POPS

Adults and kids alike will love making and eating these. Make real, all-natural ice pops and slushies using good-quality whole-leaf teas and herbal infusions. Do experiment with your favorite tea but we've given you our favorites here.

RHUBARB AND GINGER CUSTARD TWO-TONE ICE POP

MAKES 12 ICE POPS

3 cups (750ml) water
4 rhubarb and ginger tea temples
¼ cup (50g) superfine sugar
2 cups (500ml) heavy cream
1 vanilla bean
12 ice pop sticks

1 In a pan, pour in the measured water and bring to a boil. Pop in the tea temples, remove from the heat, and let steep for 5 minutes. Squeeze out the tea temples and discard, then stir in 2 tablespoons of the sugar until it has dissolved. Let cool and then chill completely.

2 Pour the cream and the remaining sugar into a pan along with the vanilla bean and bring slowly to a boil, making sure the sugar dissolves. Cover and let cool completely, then remove the vanilla bean.

3 Place 12 x 3-ounce (75-ml) ice pop molds in their holders in the freezer and pour the rhubarb tea mixture into each mold, about halfway up the mold, then freeze. (If you're feeling quirky, then prop the molds at different angles to get a more interesting design once they're frozen.) When solid, pour the custard mixture on top (just below the top to allow for expansion) and freeze again. When they're half frozen (after about 1 to 2 hours), add a ice pop stick to each and return to the freezer until completely solid.

SUPERFRUIT TEA ICE POPS WITH EDIBLE FLOWERS

MAKES 10 ICE POPS

3 cups (750ml) water
scant ½ cup (100g) honey
2 tablespoons superfruit (or hibiscus
    with mixed berries) whole leaf tea
juice of ½ lemon
edible flowers or petals (such as rose
    petals, small pansies, or violas)
10 ice pop sticks

1 In a pan, pour in the measured water and bring to a boil. Pour into a measuring cup, stir in the honey and tea leaves, and let steep for 5 minutes, then strain and add the lemon juice. Let cool and then chill completely.

2 Pour a little liquid into each of 10 x 3-ounce (75-ml) ice pop molds and add a couple of small edible flowers or petals.

3 Place the molds in the freezer and freeze until solid then add more flowers and more tea and continue this freezing and topping off process to have suspended flowers throughout the ice pop until all the tea mixture has been used (finish off just below the top of the molds to allow for expansion). Be sure to add a ice pop stick to each ice pop at the last layer. Freeze until solid.

LEMON AND GINGER TEA ICE POPS

**MAKES 10 ICE POPS/
SERVES 8 AS A SLUSHY**

3 cups (750ml) water
scant ½ cup (100g) honey
6 tablespoons lemon and ginger
    whole leaf tea
finely grated zest
    and juice of
    1 lemon
10 ice pop sticks
(optional)

1 In a pan, pour in the measured water and bring to a boil. Pour into a measuring cup, stir in the honey, tea leaves, and lemon zest, and let steep for 5 minutes, then strain and add the lemon juice. Let cool and then chill completely.

2 Pour the liquid into each of 10 x 3-ounce (75-ml) ice pop molds (just below the top of the molds to allow for expansion) and pop in the freezer; freeze for 1 to 2 hours or until half set, then add a ice pop stick to each mold and return to the freezer until solid.

3 If you want to make the slushy, then pour the mixture into a 10 x 6-inch (25 x 15-cm) cake pan. Place in the freezer and freeze for about an hour or until ice crystals are forming around the rim and on the bottom of the pan. Scrape the mixture with a fork, combining well with any liquid, then return to the freezer. Repeat every 45 minutes or so until you see uniform crystals forming (it'll take about 3 to 4 hours in total). Spoon the flakes of slushy into pretty glasses to serve.

BLACK CURRANT TEA AND CHOCOLATE TRUFFLE ICE CREAM

There's something about the slightly smoky, potent, and fruity flavor of black currant tea that makes it the perfect complement to chocolate as in this recipe from David Lebovitz's book *The Perfect Scoop*. If you prefer more fragrant teas, then switch the black currant tea leaves below to loose-leaf Earl Grey, Tung Ting oolong, or superfruit (hibiscus with mixed berries) instead.

MAKES ABOUT 4 CUPS (1 LITER)

FOR THE CHOCOLATE TRUFFLES
⅔ cup (140ml) heavy cream
3 tablespoons corn or glucose syrup
6 ounces (170g) semisweet chocolate
    (45% minimum cocoa solids),
    chopped
1 teaspoon cognac, rum, or other
    liqueur

FOR THE ICE CREAM
1 cup (250ml) whole milk
¾ cup (150g) sugar
½ ounce/10 tsp 15g) black currant
    whole leaf tea (or another tea,
    see intro)
2 cups (500ml) heavy cream
5 large egg yolks

1 First, make the truffles. Heat the cream with the corn or glucose syrup in a small pan until it just begins to boil. Remove from the heat and add the chocolate, stirring until it's melted and the mixture is smooth. Mix in the alcohol. Scrape the mixture into a small bowl and freeze until firm, about 1 hour.

2 Line a dinner plate with plastic wrap. Form little ¾-inch (2-cm) truffles using 2 small spoons; you can, of course, make them bigger or smaller depending on what takes your fancy. Scoop up a teaspoonful of truffle mixture, then scrape it off with the other spoon onto the dinner plate. Repeat, using all the truffle mix. Freeze the truffles until ready to mix into the ice cream. These truffles can be refrigerated or frozen, well wrapped, for up to 2 weeks.

3 Now, for the ice cream. Warm the milk, sugar, tea leaves, and half of the cream in a medium pan. Cover, remove from the heat and let steep at room temperature for 1 hour.

4 Rewarm the tea-infused milk. Pour the remaining cream into a large bowl and set a strainer on top. You'll need a large bowl of iced water too.

5 In a separate bowl, whisk the egg yolks. Slowly pour the warm mixture into the egg yolks, whisking constantly, then scrape the warmed egg yolks back into the pan.

6 Stir the mixture constantly over medium heat with a heatproof spatula, scraping the bottom as you stir, until the mixture thickens and coats the spatula. Next, pour the custard through the strainer into the bowl of cream, pressing gently on the tea leaves to extract the maximum flavor from them; then discard the leaves. Stir the mixture until cool over an ice bath.

7 Chill the mixture thoroughly in the refrigerator, then freeze it in an ice-cream maker according to the manufacturer's directions. If you don't have an ice-cream maker, freeze the mixture in a tub and be sure to get it out of the freezer and vigorously stir it at regular intervals (a whisk or sturdy spatula should do the trick) to avoid icy particles forming in the ice cream. It'll take 2 to 3 hours to freeze this way in the freezer.

8 When the ice cream is ready, fold three-quarters of the chocolate truffles into the ice cream as you remove it from the ice-cream maker (or the freezer). If you wish, chop the chilled truffles into smaller pieces first. Roll the remaining chocolate truffles in unsweetened cocoa to serve on the side.

SIPSMITH SUPERFRUIT SUNDOWNER

Our friends over at Sipsmith in London have come up with a fab new recipe idea, using tea! We recommend you make the most of the last summer days with a nice fruity tipple.

SERVES 1

2 orange wedges
2 lemon wedges
1 grapefruit wedge
scant ¼ cup (40ml) Sipsmith London Dry Gin
1 tablespoon (25ml) superfruit tea syrup (see below)
orange twist, to garnish

FOR THE SUPERFRUIT TEA SYRUP

2 cups (500ml) water
2½ cups (500g) sugar
3 to 4 superfruit tea temples (or hibiscus with mixed berries whole leaf mesh tea bags)

1 First, make the tea syrup by combining the water and sugar in a pan. Bring to a simmer and stir until the sugar has dissolved. Remove from the heat and add the tea temples or mesh bags. Let the liquid rest until it reaches room temperature (about 30 minutes). Then, remove and discard the tea temples (or mesh bags) and transfer the liquid to a sterilized bottle and keep in the refrigerator until you're ready to use it.

2 Now, to make the drink. Fill a cocktail shaker with ice. Squeeze orange and lemon wedges into it. Squeeze the grapefruit wedge and drop it into the shaker. Add the gin and tea syrup. Shake well. Strain into a chilled cocktail glass and garnish with an orange twist.

OLD WILLIAMSBURG MANDARIN TEA

This punch recipe from *The Williamsburg Art of Cookery* (see also page 73) has been tweaked by food writer Lindy Wildsmith in her book *Artisan Drinks*, who says it makes a great after-dinner drink. Not strictly a liqueur, this tipple is for impatient liqueur-makers who want a drink to make and consume straightaway; although, it has to be said, if you can hold back it does improves with age.

MAKES 4 CUPS (1 LITER)

juice and rind of 2 mandarins
1 cup (225ml) any strong tea, cooled
juice of 1 extra mandarin
juice and thinly pared rind of 1 lemon
⅔ cup (125g) packed raw brown or granulated sugar
1¼ cups (300ml) top-quality rum

1 You'll need to source a couple of large bottles or Mason jars to fit 4 cups (1 liter) of liquid in.

2 Start by scraping the pith off the back of the mandarin rind, put all the ingredients in the bottle or jar, and seal. Shake well until the sugar dissolves. Leave overnight and strain through a strainer lined with cheesecloth into a second bottle and drink when the spirit moves you.

3 Once made, this drink keeps for six months or more.

Variation: The original Williamsburg version used the thinly pared rind and juice of 2 lemons instead of mandarins; if you would like to try this version, then you may want to add a little more sugar, to taste.

ALMOND ICED TEA

This drink, created by mixologist Dre Masso for Beefeater 24's specific flavors, featured in Tom Sandham's book *World's Best Cocktails*. It uses Sencha tea but we think Matcha or another green tea could work well, too. The almond in the orgeat syrup complements the herbal notes of the green tea.

SERVES 1

ice cubes
scant ¼ cup (50ml) Beefeater 24 gin
3 teaspoons lemon juice
scant ½ cup (100ml) chilled Sencha or
*   Mao Feng green tea*
4 teaspoons orgeat syrup (a sweet and
fragrant syrup made from almonds,
*   sugar, and rose water or orange*
*   flower water)*
slice of lemon

1 Pour all the ingredients into a glass over ice and stir. Garnish with a lemon wheel.

SPICED WINTER MULLED WINE

Spiced winter tea is like Christmas in a cup! Rooibos tea, cinnamon, cloves, and orange peel—these flavors are pretty much everything you need to make a gorgeous mulled wine (well, almost everything you need), now where's that bottle of red ...

MAKES 4 CUPS (1 LITER)

*5 spiced winter tea temples
(or winter-spiced rooibos whole
leaf mesh tea bags)
3 cups (750ml) good
quality red wine
1 cup (250ml) water
4 tablespoons sugar
½ orange, sliced
ginger cookies,
to serve (optional)*

1 Snip the strings off the tea temples (or mesh bags, if using) and simply throw all of the ingredients into one big pan. Bring to just below boiling point, stirring occasionally.

2 Then, turn the heat right down and simmer for 10 minutes.

3 Serve warm, not too hot, as a delicious, warming drink on a cold day!

EARL GREY MARTINI WITH A LEMON SALT RIM

This martini is a classic, sophisticated kind of cocktail. Tea is often used by mixologists in cocktails—it is tasty and refreshing. Here's how to make your own at home.

SERVES 1

FOR THE EARL GREY SYRUP
4 tablespoons water
2 tablespoons Earl Grey strong whole leaf tea
3 tablespoons superfine sugar

FOR THE LEMON SALT RIM
finely grated zest of 2 lemons
⅓ cup (50g) sea salt

FOR THE MARTINI
2 tablespoons gin
1 tablespoon lemon juice
ice cubes

FOR THE GARNISH
a long piece of lemon peel tied in a knot
dried borage flowers, picked from the Earl Grey strong tea leaves

1 First, make the Earl Grey syrup by heating the water in a small pan, stir in the tea leaves and sugar and stir until the sugar has dissolved. Remove from the heat and let infuse for 10 minutes, then strain and chill.

2 Chill the martini glass. Meanwhile, whiz the lemon zest and salt until very fine and transfer to a shallow dish or saucer.

3 For each martini, dip the chilled glass into the lemon salt, then pour the gin, Earl Grey syrup, and lemon juice into a cocktail shaker with ice, shake well, then strain into the glass and garnish with the lemon knot and sprinkle with the dried borage flowers.

MATCHARITA

This twist on the Margarita, from bartender Ago Perrone (of the Connaught Bar, Mayfair, London) and mixologist Tom Sandham from his book *World's Best Cocktails*, uses Matcha for a modern feel and adds a touch of Zen to the cocktail ceremony.

SERVES 1

3½ tablespoons Calle 23 tequila blanco
2 teaspoons orange curaçao
4 teaspoons unsalted yuzu juice
2 teaspoons maraschino liqueur
¼ teaspoon brewed Matcha tea
ice cubes
black salt and lemon slices, to garnish

1 Shake all the ingredients with ice and serve straight up in a glass (or even a teacup) with lemon slices sprinkled with black salt.

SUPEREASY, REAL, FRESHLY BREWED ICED TEAS

Forget those sugary, bottled iced teas you might have tried before. Freshly brewed iced teas made with real ingredients are just so much tastier and better for you. If you use good-quality ingredients, it takes just minutes for the flavors to come through. All teas taste great iced. You can use any black, green, white, or oolong teas; or try fruit and herbal blends to make caffeine-free iced teas. If they contain real, whole pieces of fruit and herbs, they will give you lots and lots of flavor—it's a bit like making your own cordial. Below we share how to make our superfresh iced tea. Oh and did we say, these are all very low calorie too? Hurrah!

SERVES 1

1 tea temple (or 2 teaspoons whole
  leaf tea)
1 cup (250ml) freshly boiled water
ice cubes
fresh fruit, to garnish
agave nectar (optional)

1 Take 1 tea temple (or whole leaf tea, if using) per person or per 1-cup (250-ml) glass (or supersize the recipe to make a 4-cup/1-liter pitcher for sharing) and pour in freshly boiled water so that it just covers the tea temple or whole leaf tea (about 1 inch/2.5cm high). Let brew for 5 minutes then top with cold water and ice cubes; remember to strain out the tea leaves, if using, before the next step or just strain before serving, it's up to you.

2 Next, add some fresh fruit for extra flavor and prettiness. Lemons and limes go well with traditional teas and red berries and passion fruit taste amazing with fruit and herbal teas.

3 You can take the tea temple out of the pitcher if you like, but we like to keep it in; it will continue to infuse and you can just keep topping off with ice.

4 If you like a sweeter tea, then add a squirt of agave nectar (an all-natural sweetener) along with the boiling water.

Our favorite ice tea combos:

The classic one—Darjeeling Earl Grey tea, a squeeze of fresh lemon juice, and some lemon slices, for decoration

The elegant one—Mao Feng green tea, a handful of cucumber and lime slices, and 3 to 4 mint leaves

The "woah, that's a lot of flavor" one—licorice and mint tea. Straight up. The peppermint leaves and the licorice give you lots of natural flavor and sweetness.

The fruity one—superfruit tea (hibiscus with mixed berries),
2 handfuls of fresh berries, the fruit of 2 passion fruits.
You'll never need to buy cordial again!

ICED TEA ON THE GO? If you give them a little more time, tea will infuse in cold water. So, add a tea temple (or whole leaf tea) to your "on the go" water bottle before you leave home. The tea will infuse and you'll have an all-natural, delicious iced-tea flavored-water throughout the day.

"KNOCK YOUR SOCKS OFF" TEA SHAKES

Tea and milk shakes. Not exactly an obvious combination but, if you give these a go, we're sure you'll agree we're on to something! Because they contain real ingredients (pieces of fruit, spices, chocolate, caramel) quality whole leaf teas give you intense flavor and these tea shakes will literally blow your socks off (that's a warning by the way).

SERVES 1

1 tea temple (or 2 teaspoons whole leaf tea (or more depending on how strong you like your flavor!))
scant ½ cup (100ml) freshly boiled water
3 scoops good-quality vanilla ice cream
milk, to thin the consistency, if necessary

1 Pop a tea temple (or whole leaf tea, if using) into a cup and add the water. Let brew for 10 minutes; you could leave it longer if you like your flavors superstrong.

2 Once brewed, remove and discard the tea temple (or tea leaves, if using), and pour the liquid into a blender. Add 3 scoops of ice cream and blend some more. If the mixture is too thick, then pour in a little skim or lowfat milk and blend again. Drink. Smile.

• •

As ever, we're big fans of experimenting, so do give this method a go with your favorite tea blend , but here are our four most favorite, tried and tested, "Oh wow these are good" tea shakes:

Chocolate and mint
Superfruit
Darjeeling Earl Grey
Rooibos crème caramel

• •

MATCHA COCONUT TEA SHAKE

We're always banging up about Matcha's superpower because it is, well, super. But Matcha also tastes amazing and sometimes we like to just indulge in that, so here is an extremely yummy and very creamy Matcha tea shake recipe. Oh, and if you're not a fan of coconut then vanilla or white chocolate ice cream also are dreamy with Matcha.

SERVES 1

scant ½ cup (100ml) skim milk
3 scoops coconut-flavoured ice cream
1 teaspoon Matcha

1 Put the milk and ice cream into a blender, then add the Matcha. Blend. Drink. Grin.

Top Tip Always add liquids into the blender before the Matcha powder as the Matcha has a tendency to stick to the sides of the blender otherwise.

• •

Feeling extra indulgent? You could add:

some whipped cream
some chocolate sauce
some slivered almonds
a fresh mint leaf for fanciness.

• •

ALL-NATURAL CHAI AND MATCHA LATTES

We talked earlier about chai tea (see page 54), and how this spicy, milky, and sweet black tea is made and drunk throughout India and its neighbors. The modern Western chai is often made using instant tea powders and/or spice-flavored syrups, which can be cloyingly sweet and aren't very natural. We suggest you make your own chai lattes using whole leaf chai tea; you'll be amazed at the yummy, warming, spicy, indulgent flavor you'll get. And you'll be pleased to know, it takes just a few minutes.

CHAI LATTES

SERVES 1

1 chai tea temple (or 2 teaspoons chai whole leaf tea)
freshly boiled water, to cover
1 teaspoon raw brown sugar
generous ¾ to 1 cup (200 to 250ml) skim or lowfat milk (dependent on cup/glass size)
a sprinkle of ground cinnamon, to taste

1 Pop a chai tea tea temple (or whole leaf tea, if using) in a mug or latte glass and pour in freshly boiled water so that it just covers the tea temple (about 1 inch/2.5cm high) or tea leaves.

2 Add the sugar (or more/less to taste); if you prefer, use honey or agave syrup as sweeteners. Let brew for 3 to 5 minutes and then discard the tea. You can leave the tea temple in (it'll continue to infuse) or take it out if you prefer; if using whole leaf tea, do strain out the tea leaves.

3 In the meantime, make your hot, frothy milk. If you have a coffee machine with a steamer, you can use that. Otherwise, heat your milk in the microwave or on the stove and use a handheld whisk to get it frothy and transfer to your mug or glass. Top with a sprinkle of cinnamon, to taste, and enjoy.

ALMOND MATCHA LATTE

SERVES 1

1 teaspoon Matcha
a little not-quite-boiled water*
a squirt of agave nectar
a sprinkle of ground cinnamon and
   a grating of nutmeg
¾ to 1 cup (200 to 250ml) almond
   milk (dependent on cup size)

• •

Why not try?

Swap ingredients around to make this work for you and your taste buds. Here are swaps we've tried:
• **cow's milk (lowfat or skim) instead of almond milk**
• **coconut milk, oat milk, rice milk, and other dairy-free alternatives all work well instead of almond milk**
• **½ teaspoon of vanilla extract, sugar or coconut sugar to sweeten, instead of the agave nectar.**

• •

1 In a mug, make a paste of the Matcha and water* using a handheld whisk (the small electric kind works well). *Temperature! Ideally, because Matcha is a green tea, the water you use shouldn't be boiling, it should be about 176°F (80°C). Unless you have a fancy kettle that boils at different temperatures, you're unlikely to be able to heat your water so precisely, so you should just click your kettle off before it boils or let it sit for a few minutes after it's boiled. That way, the temperature will be just right.

2 Next, add the agave nectar and spices.

3 Now, make your almond milk hot and frothy. If you have a coffee machine with a steamer, you can use that. Otherwise, heat your milk in the microwave or on the stove and use a handheld whisk to get it nice and frothy.

4 Transfer the milk to your mug, mix with the Matcha paste, drink, and enjoy the sprightliness that will come.

PREFER LOOSE? If you like to use loose-leaf tea then you could always brew some chai whole leaf tea. You'll need 2 teaspoons of chai tea and to brew it for 5 minutes in about 5 tablespoons (75ml) freshly boiled water. You'll then need to strain the leaves before adding your hot frothy milk.

SUPERPOWER MATCHA SMOOTHIES

We have talked a fair bit about all the nutrients that superpower Matcha green tea contains (see page 112). The fact that it's a powder makes it a great thing to add to smoothies to make them extra healthy. So, here are four Matcha smoothies for you to try—one of them was put together for us by our friends at Jamie Oliver's Fifteen Restaurant in Old Street, London. Enjoy and feel virtuous in your healthiness!

All of these smoothies make 1 serving. You just need to put the ingredients into a blender; we find it's best to put the Matcha in last. Then you simply blend, pour into a glass, and enjoy.

MATCHA SMOOTHIE

This superdelicious smoothie was created by Fifteen Restaurant, London. It's yummy and creamy (thanks banana) yet light and fresh (thanks apple and mint), we love this smoothie at anytime of the day.

½ apple
¼ stalk celery
2 sprigs mint
½ banana
½ pear
½ tsp Matcha

MATCHA BREAKFAST BOOSTER

As the name suggests, this smoothie is great for breakfast. The oats and Matcha give you slow-release energy and the nut butter is a useful source of protein. If you're not a big fan of supersweet flavors in the morning, then you'll love this as the spinach and Matcha offer a mild, grassy taste, which we love. Feel free to substitute the whole milk for any dairy-free version if you fancy.

1¾ cups (400ml) whole milk
1 tablespoon honey
a handful of oats
1 tablespoon cashew or almond butter
a handful of spinach leaves
1 banana
½ teaspoon Matcha

DAIRY-FREE PROTEIN SMOOTHIE

Drink this sweet and creamy smoothie after exercise to help your body recover. Want to share the secret to an unbelievably creamy taste and texture in any dairy-free smoothie? Well, the answer in short is avocado! You'll be hooked after you try it. And, bonus, it tastes amazing! You could use coconut milk instead if you prefer. The fruit and Matcha offer up myriad nutrients and the hemp seeds are packed with protein—just what your body needs.

1¾ cups (400ml) almond milk
½ avocado
a handful of strawberries
a handful of raspberries
1 small mango
1 teaspoon hemp seeds
½ teaspoon Matcha

PREEXERCISE ENERGIZER

Want something sweet and earthy but light and easy to digest before a run or gym session? Then reach for a glass of this powerful smoothie. Beet juice is famed for its energizing properties and here we've combined it with Matcha and chia seeds, which have been shown to increase endurance.

scant ½ cup (100ml) beet juice
1¼ cups (300ml) coconut water
1 banana
a handful of blueberries
1 tablespoon chia seeds
½ teaspoon Matcha

Meet our teas

We make a big thing about using quality real tea—whole leaf tea, whole leaf herbs, and whole flowers. All the real ingredients are handled gently and with love, to maintain every drop of precious flavor.

EVERYDAY BREW

This is our signature blend—our daily cup, our builder's brew, our Rosy Lee. Call it what you want but our everyday brew is the ultimate British favorite. We've blended three top-quality whole leaf black teas—Assam, Ceylon, and a lovely Rwandan—to give a balanced, malty, zesty alliance and the most perfect cup of tea.
How does it taste? A gutsy tea full of flavor. We describe it as malty, zesty, and rich in strength.

DARJEELING EARL GREY

Most of the Earl Greys you find use a poor-quality black tea base from China, which is like palming yourself off as landed gentry when all you own is a Barbour jacket. In this blend we use a Darjeeling tea—the best of the best from the foothills of the Himalayas. These whole Darjeeling leaves are blended with zesty, citrus bergamot and lime flavors from the Mediterranean to create something altogether more elegant, or so we think.
How does it taste? The exotic, floral tones of Darjeeling tea are balanced with the sunny citrus taste of bergamot.

EARL GREY STRONG

Do you like your Earl Grey to come with some real oomph and wallop? Well, this is the one for you. We've blended some powerful Assam and Rwandan with the more delicate Ceylon and Darjeeling to give the perfect strong tea base to compliment the zesty bergamot. Maybe more of a Duke than a lowly Earl, what do you think?
How does it taste? Strong black tea with delicate Darjeeling and fancy bergamot. An Earl Grey but with wallop!

CHAI TEA

Every vendor, in every city, in every region of India, offers their own version of chai masala, the aromatic, spiced, milky tea that has been the Indian drink of choice for hundreds of years. Here's our version: a rich, malty Assam tea blended with cardamom pods, cinnamon, ginger, and vanilla. A satisfying, yummy drink that captures the vibrancy and color of India in a cup.
How does it taste? A gutsy Assam tea and an exotic mix of whole spices for a true taste of India.

CHILI CHAI

This blend is a twist on our traditional chai —the same authentic Indian recipe but with a little extra kick from little flakes of real chili. A gutsy Assam blended with whole cardamom pods, real chunks of ginger, cinnamon, vanilla, and not forgetting those spicy chili bits. This chai is for those of you who don't order korma and plain naan from your local curry house.
How does it taste? A gutsy Assam tea with exotic spices and an extra fiery kick at the end.

CHOCOLATE FLAKE TEA

Choccie cookies dunked in tea—a match made in heaven. Strong tea and a hint of dark, rich, chocolate—this blend gives you both. A partnership so very perfect, it belongs between the pages of a Mills and Boon novel.
How does it taste? Not sickly sweet hot chocolate, but a far more sophisticated tea and chocolate combo.

GREEN TEA WITH MINT

While haggling in the souks of Morocco, we discovered tea with mint and sugar—lots and lots of sugar! The lovely people of Morocco have their tea supersweet, this is partly because the Gunpowder green tea they drink can sometimes be a little harsh —the sweetness melts that away. After a bit of trial and error, we opted for a green tea called Chunmee or, as we prefer, Precious Eyebrows, which is a more delicate tea. Better to change the base tea than your teeth, we reckon!
How does it taste? A delicate green tea with a punchy mint taste.

JASMINE PEARLS

These tea temples house lovely little pearls of hand-rolled green tea tips which have been delicately infused with pure jasmine flowers. The leaves are just allowed to rest among the flowers to pick up their floral scent—jasmine tea doesn't get any purer than this. Once you cover with water, the leaves will unfurl from the hand-rolled pearl to reveal a whole leaf and a bud— surprisingly hypnotic viewing we think! These particular pearls are often called "dragon phoenix pearls"—that's because the tea bushes on the hillside look like a dragon coming out of the water. Although I've seen these bushes climbing the hillside I've yet to see a dragon getting out of a bath, so I can't vouch for the accuracy of this claim, unfortunately!
How does it taste? Delicate green tea with a light, floral, refreshing, natural jasmine taste.

MAO FENG GREEN TEA

If you enjoy the benefits of green tea but hate the taste, this is perfect for you. It has a delicate natural flavor of summer air, peaches, and apricots and, unlike most murky brown standard green teas, this one turns a clear, pale green when infused.
How does it taste? A delicate natural taste of fresh summer air, peaches, and apricots.

ORGANIC MATCHA

Matcha is a superhero among teas. A superconcentrated 100% green tea powder from Japan. When drinking Matcha you're swallowing and ingesting every little bit of green tea goodness. A good source of natural green tea flavonoids (catechins), amino acid L-theanine, and beta-carotene, Matcha has been drunk for centuries in Japan where it is used in the traditional tea ceremony. teapigs organic Matcha is premium grade Matcha from the Nishio region in Japan. The tea bushes are grown under lots of shade, which maximizes the chlorophyll content then hand-picked to ensure only the juicy young leaves and bud are plucked. The stems and veins are removed after which the fleshy leaves are ground by granite stones to a fine powder. This is then immediately vacuum packed and sealed to ensure maximum nutritional value is retained. That's why we call it superpower green tea.
How does it taste? With water, like a superpower green tea brew. With juice/milk, a hint of delicate green tea flavor.

POPCORN TEA

Not one we've made up, we promise! Back in the day, green tea was rather expensive and too pricey for your average Japanese peasant, so to make it go further they'd mix it with grains of toasted rice. From such humble beginnings has grown a tea that, in today's Japan, is celebrated in its own right as Genmaicha tea—or, to its friends, Popcorn tea. The British equivalent would probably be something like bubble

and squeak, although obviously not recommended for use in teapots.
How does it taste? Green tea with a popcorny, almost nutty undertone.

SILVER TIPS WHITE TEA

For two hours every morning, for a very special two weeks of the year, the tea pluckers of the Chinese Fujian province where white tea is grown, are in the fields at the crack of dawn to catch the early morning shoots. Once plucked, these are simply left in the sun to naturally wither and sent to people who appreciate this kind of thing (that'll be us at teapigs then). Possibly the most exclusive tea we stock.
How does it taste? Refreshing, light, and aromatic—think peaches and apricots. Very pure. We have chosen to bring you genuine white rather than green tea masquerading as white tea. If your white tea looks green in the cup, then it is green tea—watch out for fakes.

TUNG TING OOLONG TEA

Oolong tea, sometimes known as blue tea, is part fermented and this one—Tung Ting—takes its name from the mountainous region in Taiwan where it is grown. This area is regarded by those who know about this kind of thing—us included—as one of the finest around. We're very proud to be able to offer a genuine oolong tea, as these teas are mostly sold to the local Taiwanese at hundreds of dollars—a bit more pricey than your average cup, but worth every penny.
How does it taste? Oolong tea sits between green and black. This tea delivers the strength of a black tea, with the aromatic, flowery flavors of a green tea. Green tea is for now, but we reckon Tung Ting will be the next big thing.

APPLE AND CINNAMON

Whether its in grandma's pie, giant muffins, or American pancakes nothing beats the flavor of sweet juicy apple with punchy cinnamon spice. It's the perfect combination for a lovely fruity and spicy tea. Thanks go to the team at Olive and Bean, one of our lovely stockists in Newcastle, who suggested this blend of apple and cinnamon.
How does it taste? Like apple pie.

CHAMOMILE FLOWERS

It's long been known that the best chamomile tea comes from brewing the whole flowers. So guess what we sell? That's right, only the whole flowers of the Croatian chamomile bush. You may have noticed most other chamomile teas are made from dusty little bits—this is the crushed flowers, which, in our view, is a plain nasty thing to do. The chamomile flower is celebrated for its many benefits, which include calming and aiding sleep.
How does it taste? A beautiful yellow cup that gives way to a sweet, surprisingly juicy flavor of chamomile.

CHOCOLATE AND MINT

A classic combination. Mint choc chip ice cream, after dinner minty dark chocolates, a superretro pairing. We have put together our finest peppermint leaves and added yummy chocolate pieces to deliver a slightly indulgent drink with 3 calories per cup.
How does it taste? Like a dark chocolate mint, that you'd have after 8 p.m.

FENNEL AND LICORICE

Fennel has an aniselike aroma and is used widely around the world for both culinary and health purposes. Importantly to us it tastes yummy and is particularly delicious with its partner in crime—licorice. A naturally caffeine-free, sweet, and savory aromatic tea.
How does it taste? Super, supercleansing.

HONEYBUSH AND ROOIBOS

A scrumptious blend of slightly sweet honeybush with the nutty overtones of rooibos (Africaans for "red bush"), two native South African shrubs. They grow only in the Cederberg mountain region of South Africa and are harvested and prepared in much the same way to regular tea. Naturally caffeine-free, this blend is a great alternative to regular tea.
How does it taste? An earthy, mahogany-colored nectar that gives way to a subtly nutty flavor.

LEMON AND GINGER

Close the door to the wind and rain and brew up this all-natural, gingery, lemony brew to sweep you away to a British summer's day. Think homemade lemonade, traditional ginger beer, croquet, and morris dancers (ok, perhaps a step too far), it's simply summer in a cup. There is no match for the ginger kick and refreshing lemon in this infusion.
How does it taste? A light, refreshing burst of citrus with the subtle warmth of ginger.

PEPPERMINT LEAVES

As with our other teas, we insist that our herbal ones always use the whole leaf or flower. We think the leaf should be worshipped, not crushed. Because we use whole peppermint leaves, you'll find the flavor of this blend much stronger and fresher than regular dusty paper tea bags. Peppermint is reputed to be great for soothing sore tummies and helping us to keep a healthy digestive systems.
How does it taste? Very minty, very refreshing, very light.

PURE LEMONGRASS

Lemongrass is drunk all over Asia after meals for pure refreshment. Originally from Malaysia it flourishes in any humid clime. Commonly known as an ingredient in Thai cooking it also makes a wonderful, and unexpectedly, sweet, lime, and citrus drink.
How does it taste? An unexpectedly sweet lime and citrus drink.

RHUBARB AND GINGER

Crumble in a cup! Give us rhubarb and give us ginger, then we put them in a tea temple and here we have it; a superwow zesty rhubarb with a sweet ginger kick. Rhubarb lovers, this is for you.
How does it taste? Clean, pure, and zingy.

ROOIBOS CRÈME CARAMEL

Scrumptious, this tea has it all—rooibos is naturally caffeine-free, contains flavonoids, and is as hydrating as water. The chunks of caramel make it a sweet, rich, comforting drink to rival any dessert but a cup contains only 2 calories. We can't guarantee all temples contain caramel chunks but if you do get all 15 full of chunks, you've really hit the sweetness jackpot!
How does it taste? Woody, nutty rooibos balanced with sweet crème caramel for an indulgent, smooth, rich drink.

SPICED WINTER RED TEA

We think we've captured the best bits of winter with this one—mulled wine, mistletoe, winter coats, and rosy cheeks. Log fires, happy cats, and old movies on the TV. Tea and warming spices. This tea also makes a yummy wintery caffeine-free latte —orange, cloves, and cinnamon on a red tea base, perfect on a crisp, frosty morning.
How does it taste? Warming winter spices combined with a delicious rooibos tea base.

SUPERFRUIT

We can't get enough fruit these days and this naturally caffeine-free herbal tea is literally bursting with berries! What's more, the invigorating hibiscus flower base not only gives this tea a lovely deep red hue but a punchy and slightly tart taste.
How does it taste? Super and fruity—this cheeky drink is a little tart!

SWEET GINGER

Big in ginger flavor, loaded with sweetness and full of spice. This brew is loud, loud. Just like some other well-known folk with ginger connections.
How does it taste? Ginger, then cinnamon, then sweet.

YERBA MATE

If you've ever traveled to South America and particularly Argentina you'll see yerba mate (pronounced yerba mah-tey) being drunk by nearly everyone. Literally. Drunk to help maintain a healthy weight and for its stimulating properties, our yerba tastes a little like a smoky green tea.
How does it taste? A bit like a smoky green tea. Could this be the new lapsang souchong?

Where to drink our teas

Want to sip a cup of teapigs tea wherever you are in the world? Then, no fear as we've got a lot of countries covered. So, just pop into one of our lovely stockists, see below, and enjoy a lovely cup of tea.

(Note: information correct at time of publication.)

AUSTRIA

Coffee Pirates
Spitalgasse 17, 1090 Wien
www.kaffeepiraten.at

Feinkoch
Theobaldgasse 14,
1060 Wien
www.feinkoch.org

Motto am Fluss
Schwedenpl. 2, 1010 Wien
www.motto.at/mottoamfluss

AUSTRALIA

Holy Goat Coffee
32 Geebung Drive, Port
Macquairie, NSW 2444
www.holygoatcoffee.com.au

Hudsons Coffee
Locations nationwide
www.hudsonscoffee.com.au

Cooper's Fish and Chips
409 The Esplanade, Manly,
QLD 4179
www.facebook.com/pages/
Coopers-Fish-Chips-and-
Cafe/128719077203662

BELGIUM

Bistro Entrez
Hoogboomsteenweg 183,
2950 Kapellen
www.entrez.be

Bon Appétit
Theofiel van
Cauwenberghslei 115,
2900 Schoten
www.facebook.com/
boonappetit

Bon Appetit
Stationsstraat 88,
3150 Haacht
www.bon-appetit.be

Café Refuge
Zimmerplein 12, 2500 Lier
www.caferefugelier.be

CHINA (INCLUDING HONG KONG)
www.teapigs.hk

Blissful Carrot
85, 79 Rua Direita Carlos
Eugenio, Macau
www.facebook.com/
blissfulcarrot

Cha Cha Wan
206 Hollywood Road,
Sheung Wan, Hong Kong
www.facebook.
com/chachawan.
hongkong?fref=ts

Mr. Choi
Dessert Store
www.thechois.cc

Social & Co
Café/Bar
www.socialandco.com/cn

Village Bakery
Shop 2, G/F, Lucky Court,
16 Mui Wo Ferry Pier Road,
Mui Wo
www.facebook.com/
villagebakerylantau

YATA Limited
Various locations across
Hong Kong
www.yata.hk

DENMARK

Interflora
Locations nationwide
www.interflora.dk

Strandvejsristeriet
Kronborg 12A,
3000 Helsingør
www.strandvejsristeriet.dk

Street Coffee
Brammersgade 15,
8000 Århus
www.streetcoffee.dk

FINLAND

Cafe & Bar 21
Rovakatu 21,
96200 Rovaniemi
www.cafebar21.fi

Lapin Herkkutupa
Valtatie 37, 99100 Kittilä
www.herkkutupa.com

Malins Foodie Living
Kronvikintie 4,
65410 Vaasa
www.foodieliving.fi

Mandragora
Rovakatu 31,
96200 Rovaniemi
www.mandragora.fi

Oikaraisen Taukopaikka
Koskenkyläntie 1595,
97610 Oikarainen
www.oikaraisentaukopaikka.fi

FRANCE
www.teapigs.fr

Cosí Diva
54 rue de Seine,
75006 Paris

English Country Kitchen
4 rue Castalnau d'Auros,
33000 Bordeaux
www.englishcountrykitchen.fr

Le Petit Flottes
2 rue Cambon, 75001 Paris
www.lepetitflottes.com

Royal Mougins Spa
424 avenue du Roi,
06250 Mougins
www.royalmougins.fr

This is London
8 avenue Jean Lebas,
59100 Roubaix
www.facebook.com/pages/
This-is-London-British-food-
and-atmosphere/2640106837
88231?fref=ts

GERMANY
www.teapigs.de

Foodies
Amalienstrasse 87,
Maxvorstadt,
80799 München
www.foodies.de

N&J Food
König Adolf Platz 13,
65510 Idstein
www.nandj-food.de

GREECE

Bookabar
Agiou Konstantinou 50,
Marousi, Athens
www.bookabar.gr

Coffeebike
Pikérmion, Attiki,
Athens
www.coffeebike.net

Graffito
34 Solonos St, Athens
Centre, Kolonaki,
Athens
www.graffito.gr

Nutsural
Agiou Georgiou 12,
Chalandri 152 34,
Athens

ICELAND

GOTT restaurant
Bárustíg 11, 900
Vestmannaeyjar
www.facebook.com/
gottrestaurant

Lifandi markaður
Borgartúni 24, 105
Reykjavik
www.lifandimarkadur.is

Mosfellsbakari
Háaleltisbraut 58–60,
108 Reykjavik
www.mosfellsbakari.is

Sushibarinn
Suðurlandsbraut 10,
108 Reykjavik
www.sushibarinn.is

IRELAND

Cinnamon
83–87 Main Street,
Ranelagh, Dublin 6
www.cinnamon.ie

Jo's Café
55 Main St, Kinsale,
Co Cork
www.joskinsale.com

Market Lane Cafe Ltd
5–6 Oliver Plunkett St,
Cork City
www.marketlane.ie

The Spotty Cup Tearoom
Golden Island, Athlone,
Roscommon
www.thespottycuptearooms.ie

Urbun Café
Bray Road, Co. Dun
Laoghaire-Rathdown,
Dublin

ITALY

Castroni Ottaviano
Via Ottaviano 55,
00192, Roma
www.castroniottaviano.com

La Teiera Eclettica
Via Melzo 30, 20129 Milano
www.teieraeclettica.it

Panificio Bonci
Via Trionfale 36, 00195 Roma

Salumeria Roscioli
Via dei Guibbonari 21,
00186 Roma
www.salumeriaroscioli.com

JAPAN

café 104.5
Waterras Tower 2F,
2-101 Kandaawaji-cho,
Chiyoda-ku, Tokyo
www.cafe1045.com

Chez Kentaro (French Bistro)
247-0056 Kanagawa-ken,
Kamakura-shi, Ōfuna,
1 Chome-12-18
www.chezkentaro.com

Nakatani (pâtisserie)
6 Chome-6-27 Uehonmachi
Tennōji-ku, Ōsaka-shi,
Ōsaka-fu 543-0001
www.nakatanitei.com

Pâtisserie de Joel
Yao, Osaka
www.e-sakon.co.jp

Rose Bakery Isetan
Shinjuku
Isetan Shinjuku, 3F,
3-14-1 Shinjuku,
Shinjuku-ku,Tokyo
www.rosebakery.jp

MALAYSIA
HotShots Coffee & Tea
A2-UG1-07 Solaris Dutamas,
Jalan Dutamas 1, 50480
Kuala Lumpur
www.hotshotscoffeeandtea.com

NIGERIA
Hans and Rene
2 Abimbola Awoniyi Close,
Victoria Island, Lagos

NORWAY
Brødbakerne
Various locations
www.brodbakerne.no

Huset Glass&Interiør
Storgata 8, 8370 Leknes
www.facebook.com/
Husetglass

Jordbær Pikene
Various locations
www.jordbarpikene.no

POLAND
Barometr A2
Rynek 24, Bielsko-Biała
www.barometrcoffeeandbar.pl

Grill House
Perłowa 2, Kołobrzeg
www.grillhouse.pl

Kurhaus
Aldony 6, Wrzeszcz, Gdansk
www.facebook.com/kurhaus

Landschaft
Gimnazjalna 6, Bydgoszcz
www.facebook.com/
landschaft.store

Ministerstwo
Marszałkowska 27/35,
Warszawa
www.ministerstwokawy.pl

**RUSSIA AND
KAZAKHSTAN**
Healthy Food Cafés
Various locations
www.h-food.ru

Kuptsov Eliseevskiy
Saint Petersburg
www.kupetzeliseevs.ru

Standart Vkusa
Udaltsova 40A
www.standartvkusa.ru

Tabris Retail
Various locations
Krasnoyarsk
www.tabris.ru

Tsvetnoy Central Market
15 Building 1, Tsvetnoy
Boulevard, Moscow 127051
www.tsvetnoy.com

Zvezdniy Retail
Posadskaya ul.,
24 Yekaterinburg,
Sverdlovskaya oblast',
620102
www.uralstar.ru

SINGAPORE
Baker & Cook
77 Hillcrest Road,
Greenwood,
Singapore 288951
www.bakerandcook.biz

Cedele
252 North Bridge Road, 03-
28A Raffles City Shopping
Centre, Singapore 179103
www.cedelegroup.com

SOUTH AFRICA
Abalone House & Spa
3 Kriedoring Street,
Paternoster 7381
www.abalonehouse.co.za

The Blue Crane &
The Butterfly
146 Dorp Street,
Stellenbosch 7600
www.bluecranecoffee.co.za

Ma Mère
The Old Biscuit Mill, 375
Albert Road, Woodstock,
Cape Town 7915
www.mamere.co.za

Martins Bakery
43 Main Rd, Wynberg,
Cape Town 7800
www.martinsbakery.co.za

SPAIN
Bistrot Pastisseria
Internacional
Calle Santa Margarita 15,
17600 Figueres
www.marcjoli.com

Brunch & Cake
Calle Enric Granados 19,
08007 Barcelona
www.cupcakesbarcelona.com

Ensucrats
Calle Sant Pere 18,
43850 Cambrils
www.ensucrats.com

La Botiga del Café
Rambla Nova 88,
43001 Tarragona
www.labotigadelcafe.com

Passion Café Ibiza
Passeig Joan Carles
Primero 23, Edificio
Mediterraneo, 07800 Ibiza
www.passion-ibiza.com

SWEDEN
Blueberry
Sibyllegatan 15,
114 42 Stockholm
www.blueberrylifestyle.se

Hovås Kallbadhus
Fjordvägen 51,
436 50 Hovås
www.hovaskallbadhus.
se.loopiadns.com

Kafé Magasinet
Tredje Långgatan 9,
413 03 Goteborg
www.kafemagasinet.se

Tacos & Tequila
Tredje Långgatan 9,
413 03 Goteborg
www.tacosandtequila.se

Taverna Brillo
Sturengatan 6 ,
Humlegårdsgatan 19,
114 35 Stockholm
www.tavernabrillo.se

SWITZERLAND
Blackbird Café
Cheneau de Bourg 1,
1003 Lausanne
www.blackbirdcafe.ch

Changemaker
Various locations
www.changemaker.ch

UK
www.teapigs.co.uk

Busy Bee Garden Centre
Brading Road, Ryde,
Isle of Wight PO33 1QG
www.busybeegardencentre.
co.uk

Macbeans
2 Little Belmont Street,
Aberdeen AB10 1JG
www.macbeans.com

Milk and Sugar
10 Windsor Place,
Cardiff CF10 3BX
www.milkandsugarplease.com

Moksha Caffé
4–5 York Place. Brighton
BN1 4GY
www.mokshacaffe.com

Jersey Pottery Restaurant
5 La Colomberie, St Helier,
Jersey JE2 4QB
www.jerseypotterycafes.com

Olive and Bean
17–19 Clayton Street,
Newcastle NE1 5PN
www.oliveandbean.co.uk

Rumpus Cosie
12 Derry's Cross,
Plymouth PL1 2TE
www.radiantspace.org.uk/
rumpus-cosy

Shetland Arts Centre
Mareel, Lerwick,
Shetland Isles ZE1 0WQ
www.mareel.org

The Old Pier Tearoom
Lamlash, Brodick,
Isle of Aaran KA27 8JN

The Swan at the Globe
21 New Globe Walk,
London SE1 9DT
www.swanlondon.co.uk

UNITED ARAB EMIRATES
Ripe Fresh Farm Shop
A Street, Al Manara Street,
Near Al Manar Mosque,
Near Al Wasl Street, Dubai
www.ripeme.com

USA
www.teapigs.com

Astoria Coffee Shop
30-04 30th Street, Astoria,
NY 11102
www.astoriacoffeeny.com

Central Market
Various locations
across Texas
www.centralmarket.com

Chelsea Market Baskets
75 Ninth Avenue,
New York NY 10011
www.chelseamarketbasket.com

Fairway Market
Various locations in New York,
New Jersey and Connecticut
www.fairwaymarket.com

Forager's City Grocer
56 Adams Street, Brooklyn,
NY 11201
www.foragersmarket.com

Monsieur Marcel
1260 3rd Street Promenade,
Santa Monica CA 90404
www.mrmarcel.com

Mrs Green's Natural Market
Various locations
www.mrsgreens.com

The Dandelion
124 S 18th Street,
Philadelphia
PA 19103
www.thedandelionpub.com

The Fresh Market
Locations nationwide
www.thefreshmarket.com

The Pasta Shop
Rockridge Market Hall,
5655 College Avenue,
Suite 201, Oakland,
CA 94618
www.rockridgemarkethall.com

Index

AUTHORS' ACKNOWLEDGEMENTS

Mega, special gratitude, of course, to all teapigs, past, present and future. Thanks also to all our lovely suppliers, customers and teapigs drinkers worldwide. Huge thanks to our mums and dads for introducing us to this wonderful drink – we salute you Kilby seniors and Allen elders. And, lastly, thanks to our wonderful partners and families for sharing in almost every cup of teapigs along the way.

PUBLISHER'S ACKNOWLEDGEMENTS

The publisher would like to thank the following for allowing them to reproduce these recipes:
Tea-smoked duck breasts with spiced pears (see page 164) from *Cured* and Old Williamsburg Mandarin Tea (see page 188) from *Artisan Drinks*, both by Lindy Wildsmith. Earl Grey Hearts (see page 169) by Alison Walker of Hearst Magazines/Country Living, from *Handmade Gifts from the Kitchen*. Green Tea Pound Cake (see page 173) and Jewish Honey Cake (see page 178) by Roger Pizey, from *World's Best Cakes*. Tea Loaf (see page 174) by Jane Brocket, from *Vintage Cakes*. Blackcurrant Tea and Chocolate Truffle Ice Cream (see page 186) by David Lebovitz, from *The Perfect Scoop*. Almond Iced Tea (see page 190) and Matcharita (see page 192) by Tom Sandham, from *World's Best Cocktails*. Matcha and Chocolate Shortbread (see page 181) by William Curley, from *Couture Chocolate*.

PICTURE CREDITS

The publisher would like to thank the following sources for their kind permission to reproduce the photographs and illustrations in this book:
Page 1 Jacqui Small; 2–3 Jacqui Small; 4–5 Teapigs; 6–7 background Hong Li/Getty Images; 7 Teapigs; 8–9 background Jacqui Small; 8 top left zoryanchik/Shutterstock; 8 top right Chaitanya Deshpande; 8 bottom T Photography/Shutterstock; 9 top left Glenn Harper/Alamy; 9 left of centre Elena Dijour/Shutterstock; 9 bottom left © Grapheast / Alamy; 9 top right Scorpp/Shutterstock; 9 bottom right Daniel Farson/ Picture Post/Getty Images; 10–11 Jacqui Small; 10 top left Mvorobiev/ Dreamstime; 10 top right © Robert Harding Picture Library Ltd/Alamy; 10 bottom left © Raquel Carbonell Pagola/Alamy; 10 bottom right © FORGET Patrick/SAGAPHOTO.COM/Alamy; 11 top left Kim Walker/ Getty Images; 11 top right nattanan726/Shutterstock; 11 bottom left Johnny Haglund/Lonely Planet Images/Getty Images; 11 bottom right © Thomas Lehne/ lotuseaters/Alamy; 12–13 Jacqui Small; 14–15 Teapigs; 22 © Luke Martley/Alamy; 23 top left © Tony French/Alamy; 23 top right © Veryan Dale Alamy; 23 left of centre © Jason Plews/Alamy; 23 right of centre © Dominic Dibbs/Alamy; 23 bottom left © Robert Harding Picture Library Ltd/Alamy; 23 bottom right © Gary Roebuck/Alamy; 25 top left © Guy Bell/Alamy; 25 top right Science & Society Picture Librar/Getty Images; 25 left of centre © Illustrated London News Ltd/ Mary Evans Picture Library; 25 bottom left © Andreas von Einsiedel / Alamy; 25 bottom right Mary Evans Picture Library; 26 Andy Cox; 27 Alexa Loy/Drink, Shop & Do; 28 Tim E White/Getty Images; 29 Olivia Bryce for Greenwoods tea rooms; 30 © S. Forster/Alamy; 31 left and right Ostfriesische Tee Gesellschaft GmbH & Co.KG; 33 © Brian Jannsen/ Alamy; 36 Marten_House/Shutterstock; 37 © Iain Masterton/Alamy; 38 © Sergey Yakovlev/Alamy; 43 © Nik Wheeler/Alamy; 44 © Grapheast / Alamy; 45 © Eric Lafforgue/Alamy; 49 © Wesley/Alamy; 50 Godong/ UIG via Getty Images; 51 © Mike Hutchings/Reuters/Corbis; 55 top left © Leonid Plotkin/Alamy; 55 top right © dbimages/Alamy; 55 left of centre Alexander Mazurkevich/Shutterstock; 55 right of centre Madlen/ Shutterstock; 55 bottom left Shikhar Bhattarai/Stocksy; 55 bottom right David Pearson/Alamy; 56–57 Tuul and Bruno Morandi/Getty; 59 © dbimages/Alamy; 60 China Photos/Getty Images; 61 Song Fang Teahouse; 63 © Maksim Kostenko/Alamy; 64 Carolyn Lagattuta/Stocksy; 65 © Christophe Boisvieux/Corbis; 67 top and bottom Hotel Chinzanso; 69 © imageBROKER/Alamy; 73 Ray Kachatorian/Getty Images; 74 © age fotostock/Alamy; 75 Samovar Tea/Cesar Rubio; 78 © Bill Bachman/Alamy; 79 Thermette/Katherine Downs; 80–81 Jacqui Small; 88–89 Teapigs; 91 © Profimedia.CZ a.s./Alamy; 92 Jami Tarris/Getty Images; 94 Roberto Schnidt/AFP/Getty Images; 95 © Rick Rudnicki/Alamy; 104 background Flas100/Shutterstock; 104 Teapigs; 105 Teapigs; 106 top and bottom Teapigs; 107 Teapigs; 108 Song Fang Teahouse; 109 Teapigs, 110 Teapigs; 111 KPG_Payless/Shutterstock; 113 top and bottom Teapigs; 114 Teapigs; 115 © Cseh Ioan/Alamy; 116 top gresei/Shutterstock; 116 bottom © Bon Appetit/Alamy; 117 Teapigs; 118 top Vill Paolnen/Alamy; 118 bottom Quanthem/Shutterstock; 119 © Horizon Images/Motion/Alamy; 120 © Hailshadow/iStock; 121 J P De Manne/Robert Harding World Imagery/ Getty Images, 124 bozulek/Shutterstock; 125 © Jon Arnold Images Ltd/ Alamy; 126 Alex Nazaruk; 127 left and right Teapigs; 128 Dethan Punalor/ Stockbyte/Getty Images; 129 Teapigs; 130 Havoc/Shutterstock; 131 Gavin Thomas/Getty Images; 132 Marie-Marthe Gagnon; 133 Teapigs; 134 top left © Carol Sharp/http://www.flowerphotos.com/Eye Ubiquitous/ Corbis; 134 right Christian Jung/Shutterstock; 134 bottom left Isantilli/ Shutterstock; 135 top left Neil Overy/Gap Photos; 135 top right Lee Torrens/Shutterstock; 135 bottom left tharamust/Shutterstock; 135 bottom right ailenn/Shutterstock; 137 © Robert Harding World Imagery/Alamy; 138–139 Jaqcui Small; 140 David Hecker/AFP/Getty Images; 141 Alfred Eisenstaedt/ullstein bild via Getty Images; 143 Eitan Simanor/Getty Images; 144 © Bon Appetit/Alamy; 146 top © F1online digitale Bildagentur GmbH/Alamy; 146 bottom left © Gregory Davies/Stockimo/Alamy; 146 bottom right © YAY Media AS/Alamy; 147 top left © Adam Korzeniewski/ Alamy; 147 top right © Design Pics Inc/Alamy; 147 left of centre © SCPhotos/Alamy; 147 right of centre Stephen Morris/Stocksy; 147 bottom left © Jonathan Gordon/Alamy; 147 bottom right © Bon Appetit/ Alamy; 148–149 Matt J Eacock/Getty Images; 151 left and right Teapigs; 153 Superstock/Getty Images; 154 Renata Dobranska/Stocksy; 155 Carl Batterbee; 158–159 Teapigs; all photos pages 158–201 Jacqui Small.